From A to B & Back Again

Andy Warhol has had one-man exhibitions at galleries and museums in New York, Los Angeles, Chicago, Boston, Philadelphia, Cincinnati, Minneapolis and Pasadena, and in Paris, Buenos Aires, Milan, Stockholm, Toronto, Turin, Hamburg, Cologne, Amsterdam, Munich, Oslo, Berlin, Naples, Zurich and Geneva, including retrospectives at the Tate Gallery in 1971 and in Tokyo in 1974. His films include *Sleep*, *Kiss*, *Empire*, *Apple*, *Vinyl*, *Restaurant*, *My Hustler*, *The Velvet Underground*, *Chelsea Girls*, *Bike Boy*, *Lonesome Cowboys*, *Flesh*, *Blue Movie*, *Trash*, *Women in Revolt*, *Heat*, *Frankenstein* and *Dracula*.

He is the publisher of *Andy Warhol's Interview Magazine*.

He lives with his dog, Archie, on New York's Upper East Side.

The Philosophy of Andy Warhol

From A to B & Back Again

PICADOR published by Pan Books

First published in Great Britain 1975 by Michael
Dempsey in association with Cassell & Co. Ltd
This Picador edition published 1976 by Pan Books Ltd,
Cavaye Place, London SW10 9PG
2nd printing 1979
© Andy Warhol 1975
ISBN 0 330 24815 4
Printed and bound in Great Britain by
Richard Clay (The Chaucer Press) Ltd, Bungay, Suffolk

Dedication

To Pat Hackett, for extracting and redacting my thoughts so intelligently;

To beautiful Brigid Polk, for being on the other end;

To Bob Colacello, for getting it all together; and

To Steven M. L. Aronson, for being a great editor.

Contents

A *Just a little piece . . . . . . smaller . . . . . smaller*

B and I: How Andy
Puts His Warhol On

A I have never called my answering service.

I wake up and call B.

B is anybody who helps me kill time.

B is anybody and I'm nobody. B and I.

I need B because I can't be alone. Except when I sleep. Then I can't be with anybody.

I wake up and call B.

'Hello.'

'A? Wait and I'll turn off the TV. And pee. I took a dehydration pill and they make me pee every fifteen minutes.'

I waited for B to pee.

'Go on,' she said finally. 'I just woke up. My mouth is dry.'

'I wake up every morning. I open my eyes and think: here we go again.'

'I get up because I have to pee.'

'I never fall back to sleep,' I said. 'It seems like a dangerous thing to do. A whole day of life is like a whole day of television. TV never goes off the air once it starts for the day, and I don't either. At the end of the day the whole day will be a movie. A movie made for TV.'

'I watch television from the minute I get up,' B said. 'I look at NBC blue, then I turn to another channel and look at the background in a different color and see which way it looks better with the skin tones on the faces. I memorize some of Barbara Walters' lines so I can use them on your TV show when you get it.'

B was referring to the great unfulfilled ambition of my life: my own regular TV show. I'm going to call it *Nothing Special*.

'I wake up in the morning,' she said, 'and look at the patterns of the wallpaper. There's gray and there's a flower and there're black dots around the flower, and I'm thinking: is it Bill Blass wallpaper? It's just as famous as a painting. You know what you should do today, A? You should find the best drawer-liner paper in New York and make a portfolio out of it. Or have it made into material and go to an upholsterer and have a chair covered with it. Have the flowers tufted. And you could put accent pillows. You can do much more with a chair than you can with a painting.'

'That forty-pound shopping bag full of rice that I bought in a panic is still sitting next to my bed,' I said.

'So is mine, except it's eighty pounds and it's driving me crazy because the shopping bag doesn't match the curtains.'

'My pillow is stained.'

'Maybe you turned upside down in the middle of the night and got your period,' B said.

'I have to take off my wings.' I use five wings: one under each eye, one on either side of my mouth, and one on my forehead.

'Say that again.'

'I said I have to take off my wings.'

Was B making fun of my wings? 'Every day is a new day,' I said. 'Because I can't remember the day before. So I'm grateful to my wings.'

'Oh, Jesus,' she sighed. 'Every day *is* a new day. Tomorrow isn't that important, yesterday wasn't that important. I really am thinking about today. And the first thing I think about today is how I am going to save a buck. I wait in bed for whoever I want to call to call me. That way I save at least a dime.'

'I pop right out of bed. I shuffle, I shuttle, I tippy-toe, I cakewalk, anything to avoid the chocolate-covered cherries that are spread all over the floor like land-mines. But I always step in one. I feel the chocolate . . .'

'I CAN'T HEAR YOU. I CAN'T UNDERSTAND WHAT YOU'RE SAYING!'

'I said I realize it's a feeling I like.'

'I get up and I tip-toe. I'm afraid I'm going to wake up my houseguests it's so early, and then when I slip on a chocolate-covered cherry I really hate it, because it reminds me of putting honey on something, and then, God, the knife is dirty, and I get it on the carpet, you know how honey always drips. Honey should come out of something that squirts – like ketchup in a drive-in.'

'I crawl to the bathroom because I can't shuffle, shuttle, tippy-toe or cakewalk, with a chocolate-covered cherry caught between my toes. I approach the sink. I raise my body slowly and brace my arms against the stand.'

'I don't do that,' B said. 'I get the chocolate-covered cherry caught between my toes and then I sit in a yoga position and try to get my foot into my mouth so I can lick off the rest of the chocolate-covered cherry. Then I hop to the bathroom so I don't get any more chocolate-covered cherry on the rest of the floor. Once I get there I have to lift my leg up to the sink and take a foot-bath.'

'I'm sure I'm going to look in the mirror and see nothing. People are always calling me a mirror and if a mirror looks into a mirror, what is there to see?'

'When I look in the mirror I only know that I don't see myself as others see me.'

'Why is that, B?'

'Because I'm looking at myself the way I want to see myself. I make expressions just for myself. I don't make the expressions other people see me make. I'm not twisting my lips and saying "Money?" '

'Oh, not money, B, come on.' This B is rich so of course she has a one-track mind.

'Some critic called me the Nothingness Himself and that didn't help my sense of existence any. Then I realized that existence itself is nothing and I felt better. But I'm still obsessed with the idea of looking into the mirror and seeing no one, nothing.'

'I'm obsessed,' B said, 'with the idea of looking into the mirror and saying "I don't believe it. How can I get the publicity I get? How can I be one of the most famous persons in the world? Just look at me!" '

'Day after day I look in the mirror and I still see something – a new pimple. If the pimple on my upper right cheek is gone, a new one turns up on my lower left cheek, on my jawline, near my ear, in the middle of my nose, under the hair on my eyebrows, right between my eyes. I think it's the same pimple, moving from place to place.' I was telling the truth. If someone asked me, 'What's your problem?' I'd have to say, 'Skin.'

'I dunk a Johnson and Johnson cotton ball into Johnson and Johnson rubbing alcohol and rub the cotton ball against the pimple. It smells so good. So clean. So cold. And while the alcohol is drying I think about nothing. How it's always in style. Always in good taste. Nothing is perfect – after all, B, it's the opposite of nothing.'

'For me to think about nothing is just about impossible,' said B. 'I can't even think about it when I'm asleep. I had the worst dream of my life last night. The worst nightmare, I mean. I dreamt that I was at a meeting someplace and I had a plane reservation to come home and nobody would take me. They kept taking me to this house instead, to look at an art work for charity. I had to go up the stairs and look at all the paintings. And there was a man ahead of me and he kept saying "Turn around! You haven't seen that!" I said, "Yes, sir!" It was a curved wall going up a curved staircase, it was painted yellow, from the bottom to the top, and he said, "Well, that's the painting." I said, "Oh." Then I left with a man in a gray suit and a briefcase who went down to put another fifteen cents in the parking meter, but his car wasn't a car, it was a couch, so I knew *he* couldn't get me anyplace. That's when I tried to stop an ambulance. I wound up having to go to the party another time. Another man dragged me back to see the painting and he said, "You haven't seen everything yet." I said, "I've seen everything." He said, "But you haven't seen the man downstairs putting the fifteen cents in his car." I said, "Ha. That's not his car, it's his couch. How am I going to get to the airport on a couch?" He said, "Didn't you see him take a black notebook out of his pocket and write fifteen cents in it? He said it was the longest meeting he'd ever been to. It's a tax deduction. That's a work of art. That's his piece, putting the fifteen cents into the parking for his couch." Then I realized I didn't have any money to pay for my plane reservation – I had made and canceled it four times. So I went to a shingled house near the beach and picked up seashells. I wanted to see if I could get inside this broken seashell, and I

16

tried, A, I really tried. I got the top of my head in it and my barrette, through the hole. One strand of my hair and my barrette. I went back to the meeting and I said, "Could you please put a propeller on this man's couch, so I can get to the airport." '

This B had something on her mind. Why else would she dream like that?

'I had an awful nightmare last night too,' I said. 'I was taken to a Clinic. I was sort of involved in a charity to cheer up monsters – people who were horribly disfigured, people born without noses, people who had to wear plastic across their faces because underneath there was nothing. There was a person at the Clinic who was in charge who was trying to explain the problems these people had and their personal habits and I was just standing there and I had to listen and I just wanted it to stop. Then I woke up and I thought, "Please, please let me think about anything else. I'm just going to roll over and think about anything else that I can," and I rolled over and I dozed off and the nightmare was back! It was awful.

'The thing is to think of nothing, B. Look, nothing is exciting, nothing is sexy, nothing is not embarrassing. The only time I ever want to be something is outside a party so I can get in.'

'Three out of five parties are going to be a drag, A. I always have my car there early so I can leave if they're disappointing.'

I could have told her that if something is disappointing I know it's not nothing because nothing is not disappointing.

'When the alcohol is dry,' I said, 'I'm ready to apply the flesh-colored acne-pimple medication that doesn't resemble any human flesh I've ever seen, though it does come pretty close to mine.'

'I use a Q-tip for that,' B said. 'You know, one of the things that gets me hot is having a Q-tip in my ear. I love to clean my ears. I really find it exciting if I find a little piece of wax.'

'Okay, B, okay. So now the pimple's covered. But am I covered? I have to look in the mirror for some more clues. Nothing is missing. It's all there. The affectless gaze. The diffracted grace . . .'

'What?'

'The bored languor, the wasted pallor . . .'

'The what?'

'The chic freakiness, the basically passive astonishment, the enthralling secret knowledge . . .'

'WHAT??'

'The chintzy joy, the revelatory tropisms, the chalky, puckish mask, the slightly Slavic look . . .'

'Slightly . . .'

'The childlike, gum-chewing naïveté, the glamour rooted in despair, the self-admiring carelessness, the perfected otherness, the wispiness, the shadowy, voyeuristic, vaguely sinister aura, the pale, soft-spoken magical presence, the skin and bones . . .'

'Hold it, wait a minute. I have to take a pee.'

'The albino-chalk skin. Parchmentlike. Reptilian. Almost blue . . .'

'Stop it! I have to pee!!'

'The knobby knees. The roadmap of scars. The long bony arms, so white they look bleached. The arresting hands. The pinhead eyes. The banana ears . . .'

'The banana ears? Oh, A!!!'

'The graying lips. The shaggy silver-white hair, soft and metallic. The cords of the neck standing out around the big Adam's apple. It's all there, B. Nothing is missing. I'm everything my scrapbook says I am.'

'*Now* can I go pee, A? I'll only be a second.'

'First tell me, is my Adam's apple that big, B?'

'It's a lump in your throat. Take a lozenge.'

When B got back from peeing, we compared makeup techniques. I don't really use makeup but I buy it and I think about it a lot. Makeup is so well-advertised you can't ignore it completely. B went on for such a long time about all her 'creams' that I asked her 'Don't you like to have people come in your face?'

'Does it rejuvenate?'

'Haven't you heard about these ladies who take young guys to the theater and jerk them off so they can put it all over their face?'

'They rub it in like face cream?'

'Yes. It sort of pulls it tighter and makes them younger for the evening.'

'It does? Well, I use my own. It's better that way. That way I can do it at home before I go out for the evening. I shave my underarms, spray them, cream my face, and I'm all set for an evening.'

'I don't shave. I don't sweat. I don't even shit,' I said. I wondered what B would say to that.

'You must be full of shit, then,' she said. 'Ha ha ha.'

'After I check myself out in the mirror, I slip into my BVDs. Nudity is a threat to my existence.'

'It's not a threat to mine,' B said. 'I'm standing here now completely naked, looking at the stretch marks on my tits. Right now I'm looking at the scar on my side from my abscessed breastbone. And now I'm looking at the scar on my leg from where I fell in the garden when I was six.'

'What about *my* scars?'

'What about *your* scars?' B said. 'I'll tell you about *your* scars. I think you produced *Frankenstein* just so you could put your scars in the ad. You put your scars to work for you. I mean, why not? They're the best things you have because they're proof of something. I always think it's nice to have the proof.'

'What are they proof of?'

'You got shot. You had the biggest orgasm of your life.'

'What happened?'

'It happened so quickly it was like a flash.'

'*What* happened?'

'Remember how embarrassed you were in the hospital when the nuns saw you without your wings? And you started to collect things again. The nuns got you interested in collecting stamps, like you did when you were a kid or something. They got you interested in coins again too.'

'But you haven't told me what happened.' I wanted B to spell it out for me. If someone else talks about it, I listen, I hear the words, and I think, maybe it's all true.

'You were just lying there and Billy Name was standing over

you and crying. And you kept saying to him not to make you laugh because it really hurt.'

'And . . .? And . . .?'

'You were in a room in the intensive care unit, getting all these cards and presents from everybody, including me, but you wouldn't let me come and visit you because you thought I'd steal your pills. And you said you thought that coming so close to death was really like coming so close to life, because life is nothing.'

'Yes, yes, but how did it happen?'

'The founder of the Society for Cutting Up Men wanted you to produce a script she'd written and you weren't interested and she just came up to your work studio one afternoon. There were a lot of people there and you were talking on the telephone. You didn't know her too well and she just walked in off the elevator and started shooting. Your mother was really upset. You thought she'd die of it. Your brother was really fabulous, the one who's a priest. He came up to your room and showed you how to do needlepoint. I'd taught him how in the lobby!'

So that's how I was shot?

For some reason the idea of B and me needlepointing . . . 'After makeup, clothes make the man,' I said. 'I believe in uniforms.'

'I love uniforms! Because if there's nothing there, clothes are certainly not going to make the man. It's better to always wear the same thing and know that people are liking you for the real you and not the you your clothes make. Anyway it's more exciting to see where people live than what they wear. I mean, it's better to see their clothes hanging on their chairs than on their bodies. Everybody should just have all their clothes hanging out. Nothing should be hidden except the things you don't want your mother to see. That's the only reason I'm scared of dying.'

'Why?'

'Because my mother will come up here and find the vibrator and find the things in my diary that I've written about her.'

'I believe in bluejeans too.'

'The ones made by Levi Strauss are the best-cut, best-looking pair of pants that have ever been designed by anybody. Nobody will ever top the original bluejeans. They can't be bought old, they have to be bought new and they have to be worn in by the person. To get that look. And they can't be phoney bleached or phoney anything. You know that little pocket? It's so crazy to have that little little pocket, like for a twenty-dollar gold piece.'

'French bluejeans?'

'No, American are the best. Levi Strauss. With the little copper buttons. Studded for evening wear.'

'How do you keep them clean, B?'

'You wash them.'

'Do you iron them?'

'No, I put fabric softener. The only person who irons them is Geraldo Rivera.'

This talk of bluejeans was making me very jealous. Of Levi and Strauss. I wish I could invent something like bluejeans. Something to be remembered for. Something mass.

'I want to die with my bluejeans on,' I heard myself say.

'Oh, A,' B said impulsively, 'you should be President! If you were President, you would have somebody else be President for you, right?'

'Right.'

'You'd be just right for the Presidency. You would video-tape everything. You would have a nightly talk show – your own talk show as President. You'd have somebody else come on, the other President that's the President for you, and he would talk your diary out to the people, every night for half an hour. And that would come before the news, What the President Did Today. So there would be no flack about the President does nothing or the President just sits around. Every day he'd have to tell us what he did, if he had sex with his wife . . . You'd have to say you played with your dog Archie – it's the perfect name for the President's pet – and what bills you had to sign and why you didn't want to sign them, who was rotten to you in Congress . . . You'd have to say how many long-distance phone calls you made that day. You'd have to tell what you ate in the private dining room, and

21

you'd show on the television screen the receipts you paid for private food for yourself. For your Cabinet you would have people who were not politicians. Robert Scull would be head of Economics because he would know how to buy early and sell big. You wouldn't have any politicians around at all. You'd take all the trips and tape them. You'd play back all the tapes with foreign people on TV. And when you wrote a letter to anyone in Congress you would have it Xeroxed and sent to every paper.

'You'd be a nice President. You wouldn't take up too much space, you'd have a tiny office like you have now. You'd change the law so you could keep anything anybody gave you while you were in office, because you're a Collector. And you'd be the first nonmarried President. And in the end you'd be famous because you'd write a book: "How I Ran the Country Without Even Trying." Or if that sounded wrong, "How I Ran the Country with Your Help." That might sell better. Just think, if you were President right now, there'd be no more First Lady. Only a First Man.

'You'd have no live-in maid at the White House. A B would come in a little early to clean up. And then the other Bs would file down to Washington to see you just like they file in to see you at the Factory. It would be just like the Factory, all bulletproof. Visitors would have to get past your hairdressers. And you'd take your extra-private hairdresser with you. Can't you see her in her inflatable jacket, ready for war at any moment? Do you realize there's no reason you couldn't be President of the United States? You know all the bigwigs who could get you in, all of society, all the rich people, and that's all anyone's ever needed to get to be President. I don't know why you don't declare yourself in the running right away. Then people would know you weren't just a big joke. I want you to say every time you look at yourself in the mirror, "Politics: Washington, D.C." I mean, quit fooling around with the Rothschilds. Forget about those long trips to Montauk in the Rollses. Think about a little helicopter to Camp David. What a camp it would be. You'd have such a camp. Do you realize the opportunity of the White House? A, you've been into Politics

22

since the day I met you. You do everything in a political way. Politics can mean doing a poster that has Nixon's face on it, and says "Vote McGovern." '

'The idea was you could vote either way.'

'So, I could vote for Andy Warhol if you put Jasper Johns' face on it.'

'Sure.'

'So from now on, it's "Support Andy Warhol." '

'Well, write it in.'

'We can start the country over from scratch. We can get the Indians back on the reservations making rugs and hunting for turquoise. And we can send Rotten Rita and Ondine out to pan for gold. Can you see the Blue Room with Campbell's Soup Cans all over the walls? Because that's what Foreign Heads of State should see, Campbell's Soup Cans and Elizabeth Taylor and Marilyn Monroe. That's America. That's what should be in the White House. And you would serve Dolly Madison ice cream. A, see yourself as others see you.'

'In the Presidency?'

'Oh, it would be so nice, with your brown hat in the wintertime and Archie in your office lying on your coat.'

'Mm hmm.'

'Just think of yourself doing all the things you do in the morning – like taking off your wings – but doing it in the White House.'

'Oh, come on. We've been talking for so long I still haven't taken my wings off.'

'Flush them down the toilet.'

'Okay.'

'A, if you don't make it to the Presidency, you can become a Customs Official.'

'What? Why?'

'Remember the time you were searched at Customs. Your airline bag was loaded with candy bars, cookies, chewing gum. And they laughed. You used to eat nothing but sweets. You really have the sweetest tooth of anybody I've ever known. Now

23

you have gall-bladder problems and have to take those large white pills before every meal. I keep telling you to have it out.'

'I have to go and dye. I haven't done it yet today.'

'You spend so much time at home fiddling around with the color of your hair, eyelashes, and eyebrows. When we talk on the phone, I'm always hearing some other B yelling, in the background, "I'm going to throw out the Clairol 07!" I don't think you should throw out your dye, but I think you should dye both eyebrows the same color. When you stay home from the Factory, I think it's because your wig is out being dry-cleaned or dyed. It's always the same in back, that fluffed-up back that I always want to pat down. Sometimes I'd like to pull your wig off but somehow I can't ever do it. I know how it would hurt you.'

'Bye, B.'

I Love (Puberty)

A I like your apartment.

B It's nice, but it's only big enough for one person – or two people who are very close.

A You know two people who are very close?

At a certain point in my life, in the late 50s, I began to feel that I was picking up problems from the people I knew. One friend was hopelessly involved with a married woman, another had confided that he was homosexual, a woman I adored was manifesting strong signs of schizophrenia. I had never felt that I had problems, because I had never specifically defined any, but now I felt that these problems of friends were spreading themselves onto me like germs.

I decided to go for psychiatric treatment, as so many people I knew were doing. I felt that I should define some of my own problems – if, in fact, I had any – rather than merely sharing vicariously in the problems of friends.

I had had three nervous breakdowns when I was a child, spaced a year apart. One when I was eight, one at nine, and one at ten. The attacks – St Vitus Dance – always started on the first day of summer vacation. I don't know what this meant. I would spend all summer listening to the radio and lying in bed with my Charlie McCarthy doll and my un-cut-out cut-out paper dolls all over the spread and under the pillow.

My father was away a lot on business trips to the coal mines, so I never saw him very much. My mother would read to me in her thick Czechoslovakian accent as best she could and I would always say 'Thanks, Mom,' after she finished with Dick Tracy, even if I hadn't understood a word. She'd give me a Hershey Bar every time I finished a page in my coloring book.

When I think of my high school days, all I can remember, really, are the long walks to school, through the Czech ghetto with the babushkas and overalls on the clotheslines, in McKeesport, Pennsylvania. I wasn't amazingly popular, but I had some nice friends. I wasn't very close to anyone, although I guess I wanted to be, because when I would see the kids telling one another their problems, I felt left out. No one confided in me – I wasn't the type they wanted to confide in, I guess. We passed a bridge every day and underneath were used prophylactics. I'd always wonder out loud to everybody what they were, and they'd laugh.

I had a job one summer in a department store looking through *Vogues* and *Harper's Bazaars* and European fashion magazines for a wonderful man named Mr Vollmer. I got something like fifty cents an hour and my job was to look for 'ideas.' I don't remember ever finding one or getting one. Mr Vollmer was an idol to me because he came from New York and that seemed so exciting. I wasn't really thinking about ever going there myself, though.

But when I was eighteen a friend stuffed me into a Kroger's shopping bag and took me to New York. I still wanted to be close with people. I kept living with roommates thinking we could become good friends and share problems, but I'd always find out that they were just interested in another person sharing the rent. A t one point I lived with seventeen different people in a basement apartment on 103rd Street and Manhattan Avenue, and not one person out of the seventeen ever shared a real problem with me. They were all creative kids, too – it was more or less an Art Commune – so I know they must have had lots of problems, but I never heard about any of them. There were fights in the kitchen a lot over who had bought which slice of salami, but that was about it. I worked very long hours in those days, so I guess I wouldn't have had time to listen to any of their problems even if they had told me any, but I still felt left out and hurt.

I'd be making the rounds looking for jobs all day, and then be home drawing them at night. That was my life in the 50s: greeting cards and watercolors and now and then a coffeehouse poetry reading.

The things I remember most about those days, aside from the long hours I spent working, are the cockroaches. Every apartment I ever stayed in was loaded with them. I'll never forget the humiliation of bringing my portfolio up to Carmel Snow's office at *Harper's Bazaar* and unzipping it only to have a roach crawl out and down the leg of the table. She felt so sorry for me that she gave me a job.

So I had an incredible number of roommates. To this day almost every night I go out in New York I run into somebody I used to room with who invariably explains to my date, 'I used to live with Andy.' I always turn white – I mean whiter. After the same scene happens a few times, my date can't figure out how I could have lived with so many people, especially since they only know me as the loner I am today. Now, people who imagine me as the 60s media partygoer who traditionally arrived at parties with a minimum six-person 'retinue' may wonder how I dare to call myself a 'loner,' so let me explain how I really mean that and why it's true. At the times in my life when I was *feeling* the most gregarious and looking for bosom friendships, I couldn't find any takers, so that exactly when I was alone was when I felt the most like not being alone. The moment I decided I'd rather be alone and not have anyone telling me their problems, everybody I'd never even seen before in my life started running after me to tell me things I'd just decided I didn't think it was a good idea to hear about. As soon as I became a loner in my own mind, that's when I got what you might call a 'following'.

As soon as you stop wanting something you get it. I've found that to be absolutely axiomatic.

Because I felt I was picking up the problems of friends, I went to a psychiatrist in Greenwich Village and told him all about myself. I told him my life story and how I didn't have any problems of my own and how I was picking up my friends' problems, and he said he would call me to make another appointment so we could talk some more, and then he never called me. As I'm thinking about it now, I realize it was unprofessional of him to say he was going to call and then not call. On the way back from the psychiatrist's I stopped in Macy's and out of the blue I bought my first television set, an RCA 19-inch black and white. I brought it home to the apartment where I was living alone, under the El on East 75th Street, and right away I forgot all about the psychiatrist. I kept the TV on all the time, especially while people were telling me their problems, and the television I found to be just diverting enough so the problems people told me didn't really affect me any more. It was like some kind of magic.

My apartment was on top of Shirley's Pin-Up Bar, where Mabel Mercer would come to slum and sing 'You're So Adorable,' and the TV also put that in a whole new perspective. The building was a five-floor walk-up and originally I'd had the apartment on the fifth floor. Then, when the second floor became available, I took that, too, so now I had two floors, but not two consecutive ones. After I got my TV, though, I stayed more and more in the TV floor.

In the years after I'd decided to be a loner, I got more and more popular and found myself with more and more friends. Professionally I was doing well. I had my own studio and a few people working for me, and an arrangement evolved where they actually lived at my work studio. In those days, everything was loose, flexible. The people in the studio were there night and day. Friends of friends. Maria Callas was always on the phonograph and there were lots of mirrors and a lot of tinfoil.

I had by then made my Pop Art statement, so I had a lot of work to do, a lot of canvases to stretch. I worked from ten a.m. to ten p.m., usually, going home to sleep and coming back in the morning, but when I would get there in the morning the same people I'd left there the night before were still there, still going strong, still with Maria and the mirrors.

This is when I started realizing how insane people can be. For example, one girl moved into the elevator and wouldn't leave for a week until they refused to bring her any more Cokes. I didn't know what to make of the whole scene. Since I was paying the rent for the studio, I guessed that this somehow was actually *my* scene, but don't ask me what it was all about, because I never could figure it out.

The location was great – 47th Street and Third Avenue. We'd always see the demonstrators on their way to the UN for all the rallies. The Pope rode by on 47th Street once on his way to St Patrick's. Khrushchev went by once, too. It was a good, wide street. Famous people had started to come by the studio, to peek at the on-going party, I suppose – Kerouac, Ginsberg, Fonda and Hopper, Barnett Newman, Judy Garland, the Rolling Stones. The Velvet Underground had started rehearsing in one part of the loft, just before we got a mixed-media roadshow together and started our cross-country in 1963. It seemed like everything was starting then.

The counterculture, the subculture, pop, superstars, drugs, lights, discothèques – whatever we think of as 'young-and-with-it' – probably started then. There was always a party somewhere: if there wasn't a party in a cellar, there was one on a roof, if there wasn't a party in a subway, there was one on a bus; if there wasn't one on a boat, there was one in the Statue of Liberty. People were always getting dressed up for a party. 'All Tomorrow's Parties' was the name of a song the Velvets used to do at the Dom when the Lower East Side was just beginning to shake off its immigrant status and get hip. 'What costumes shall the poor girl wear / To all tomorrow's parties . . .' I really liked that song. The Velvets played it and Nico sang it.

In those days everything was extravagant. You had to be rich to be able to afford pop clothes from boutiques like Paraphernalia or from designers like Tiger Morse. Tiger would go down to Klein's and Mays and buy a two-dollar dress, tear off the ribbon and flower, bring it up to her shop, and sell it for four hundred dollars. She had a way with accessories, too. She'd paste a ditsy on something from Woolworth's and charge fifty dollars for it. She had an uncanny talent for being able to tell which people who came into her shop were actually going to buy something. I once saw her look for a second at a nice-looking well-dressed lady and say, 'I'm sorry, there's nothing for sale for you here.' She could always tell. She would buy anything that glittered. She was the person who invented the electric-light dress that carried its own batteries.

In the 60s everybody got interested in everybody else. Drugs helped a little there. Everybody was equal suddenly – debutantes and chauffeurs, waitresses and governors. A friend of mine named Ingrid from New Jersey came up with a new last name, just right for her new, loosely defined show-business career. She called herself 'Ingrid Superstar'. I'm positive Ingrid invented that word. At least, I invite anyone with 'superstar' clippings that predate Ingrid's to show them to me. The more parties we went to, the more they wrote her name in the papers, Ingrid Superstar, and 'superstar' was starting its media run. Ingrid called me a few weeks ago. She's operating a sewing machine now. But her name is still going. It seems incredible, doesn't it?

In the 60s everybody got interested in everybody.
In the 70s everybody started dropping everybody.
The 60s were Clutter.
The 70s are very empty.

When I got my first TV set, I stopped caring so much about having close relationships with other people. I'd been hurt a lot to the degree you can only be hurt if you care a lot. So I guess I did care a lot, in the days before anyone ever heard of 'pop art' or 'underground movies' or 'superstars.'

So in the late 50s I started an affair with my television which has continued to the present, when I play around in my bedroom with as many as four at a time. But I didn't get married until 1964 when I got my first tape recorder. My wife. My tape recorder and I have been married for ten years now. When I say 'we', I mean my tape recorder and me. A lot of people don't understand that.

The acquisition of my tape recorder really finished whatever emotional life I might have had, but I was glad to see it go. Nothing was ever a problem again, because a problem just meant a good tape, and when a problem transforms itself into a good tape it's not a problem any more. An interesting problem was an interesting tape. Everybody knew that and performed for the tape. You couldn't tell which problems were real and which problems were exaggerated for the tape. Better yet, the people telling you the problems couldn't decide any more if they were really having the problems or if they were just performing.

During the 60s, I think, people forgot what emotions were supposed to be. And I don't think they've ever remembered. I think that once you see emotions from a certain angle you can never think of them as real again. That's what more or less has happened to me.

I don't really know if I was ever capable of love, but after the 60s I never thought in terms of 'love' again.

However, I became what you might call *fascinated* by certain people. One person in the 60s fascinated me more than anybody I had ever known. And the fascination I experienced was probably very close to a certain kind of love.

2 **Love (Prime)**

A Should we walk? It's really beautiful out.
B No.
A Okay.

Taxi was from Charleston, South Carolina – a confused, beautiful debutante who'd split with her family and come to New York. She had a poignantly vacant, vulnerable quality that made her a reflection of everybody's private fantasies. Taxi could be anything you wanted her to be – a little girl, a woman, intelligent, dumb, rich, poor – anything. She was a wonderful, beautiful blank. The mystique to end all mystiques.

She was also a compulsive liar; she just couldn't tell the truth about anything. And what an actress. She could really turn on the tears. She could somehow always make you believe her – that's how she got what she wanted.

Taxi invented the mini-skirt. She was trying to prove to her family back in Charleston that she could live on nothing, so she would go to the Lower East Side and buy the cheapest clothes, which happen to be little girls' skirts, and her waist was so tiny she could get away with it. Fifty cents a skirt. She was the first person to wear ballet tights as a complete outfit, with big earrings to dress it up. She was an innovator – out of necessity as well as fun – and the big fashion magazines picked up on her look right away. She was pretty incredible.

We were introduced by a mutual friend who had just made a fortune promoting a new concept in kitchen appliances on television quiz shows. After one look at Taxi I could see that she had more problems than anybody I'd ever met. So beautiful but so sick. I was really intrigued.

She was living off the end of her money. She still had a nice Sutton Place apartment, and now and then she would talk a rich friend into giving her a wad. As I said, she could turn on the tears and get anything she wanted.

In the beginning I had no idea how many drugs Taxi took, but as we saw more and more of each other it began to dawn on me how much of a problem she had.

Next in importance for her, after taking the drugs, was having the drugs. Hoarding them. She would hop in a limousine and make a run to Philly crying the whole way that she had no amphetamines. And somehow she would always get them because there was just something about Taxi. Then she would add it to the pound she had stashed away at the bottom of her footlocker.

One of her rich sponsor-friends even tried to set her up in the fashion business, designing her own line of clothes. He'd bought a loft on 29th Street outright from a schlock designer who had just bought a condominium in Florida and wanted to leave the city fast. The sponsor-friend took over the operation of the whole loft with the seven seamstresses still at their machines and brought Taxi in to start designing. The mechanics of the business were all set up, all she had to do was come up with designs that were basically no more than copies of the outfits that she styled for herself.

She wound up giving 'pokes' to the seamstresses and playing with the bottles of beads and buttons and trimmings that the previous manager had left lining the wall. The business, needless to say, didn't prosper. Taxi would spend most of the day at lunch uptown at Reuben's ordering their Celebrity Sandwiches – the Anna Maria Alberghetti, the Arthur Godfrey, the Morton Downey were her favorites – and she would keep running into the ladies' room and sticking her finger down her throat and throwing each one up. She was obsessed with not getting fat. She'd eat and eat on a spree and then throw up and throw up, and then take four downers and pop off for four days at a time. Meanwhile her 'friends' would come in to 'rearrange' her pocketbook while she was sleeping. When she'd wake up four days later she'd deny that she'd been asleep.

At first I thought that Taxi only hoarded drugs. I knew that hoarding is a kind of selfishness, but I thought it was only with the drugs that she was that way. I'd see her beg people for enough for a poke and then go and file it in the bottom of her footlocker in its own little envelope with a date on it. But I finally realized that Taxi was selfish about absolutely everything.

38

One day when she was still in the designing business a friend and I went to visit her. There were scraps and scraps of velvets and satins all over the floor and my friend asked if she could have a piece just large enough to make a cover for a dictionary she owned. There were thousands of scraps all over the floor, practically covering our feet, but Taxi looked at her and said, 'The best time is in the morning. Just come by in the morning and look through the pails out front and you'll probably find something.'

Another time we were riding in a cab and she was crying that she didn't have any money, that she was poor, and she opened her pocketbook for a Kleenex and I happened to catch sight of one of those clear plastic change purses all stuffed with green. I didn't bother to say anything. What was the point? But the next day I asked her, 'What happened to that clear plastic change purse you had yesterday that was stuffed with money?' She said, 'It was stolen last night at a discothèque.' She couldn't tell the truth about anything.

Taxi hoarded brassières. She kept around fifty brassières – in graduated shades of beige, through pale pink and deep rose to coral and white – in her trunk. They all had the price tags on them. She would never remove a price tag, not even from the clothes she wore. One day the same friend that asked her for the scrap of material was short on cash and Taxi owed her money. So she decided to take a brassière that still had the Bendel's tags on it back to the store and get a refund. When Taxi wasn't looking she stuffed it into her bag and went uptown. She went to the lingerie department and explained that she was returning the bra for a friend – it was obvious that this girl was far from an A-cup. The saleslady disappeared for ten minutes and then came back holding the bra and some kind of a log book and said, 'Madame. This bra was purchased in 1956.' Taxi was a hoarder.

Taxi had an incredible amount of makeup in her bag and in her footlocker: fifty pairs of lashes arranged according to size, fifty mascara wands, twenty mascara cakes, every shade of Revlon shadow ever made – iridescent and regular, matte and shiny –

twenty Max Factor blush-ons . . . She'd spend hours with her makeup bags Scotch-taping little labels on everything, dusting and shining the bottles and compacts. Everything had to look perfect.

But she didn't care about anything below the neck.

She would never take a bath.

I would say, 'Taxi. Take a bath.' I'd run the water and she would go into the bathroom with her bag and stay in there for an hour. I'd yell, 'Are you in the tub?' 'Yes, I'm in the tub.' Splash splash. But then I'd hear her tip-toeing around the bathroom and I'd peek through the keyhole and she'd be standing in front of the mirror, putting on more makeup over what was already caked on her face. She would never put water on her face – only those degreasers, those little tissue-thin papers you press on that remove the oils without ruining the makeup. She used those.

A few minutes later I'd peek through the keyhole again and she'd be recopying her address book – or somebody else's address book, it didn't matter – or else she'd be sitting with a yellow legal pad making the list of all the men she'd ever been to bed with, dividing them into three categories – 'Slept', 'Fucked', and 'Cuddled'. If she made a mistake on the last line and it looked messy, she'd tear it off and start all over. After an hour she'd come out of the bathroom and I'd say, gratuitously, 'You didn't take a bath.' 'Yes. Yes I did.'

I slept in the same bed with Taxi once. Someone was after her and she didn't want to sleep with him, so she crawled into bed in the next room with me. She fell asleep and I just couldn't stop looking at her, because I was so fascinated-but-horrified. Her hands kept crawling, they couldn't sleep, they couldn't stay still. She scratched herself constantly, digging her nails in and leaving marks. In three hours she woke up and said immediately that she hadn't been asleep.

Taxi drifted away from us after she started seeing a singer-musician who can only be described as The Definitive Pop Star – possibly of all time – who was then fast gaining recognition on

40

both sides of the Atlantic as the thinking man's Elvis Presley. I missed having her around, but I told myself that it was probably a good thing that he was taking care of her now, because maybe he knew how to do it better than we had.

Taxi died a few years ago in Hawaii where an important industrialist had taken her for a 'rest'. I hadn't seen her for years.

3 Love (Senility)

B Why didn't you show up last night? You've been in a funny mood lately.

A It's just – I can't meet new people. I'm too tired.

B Well, these were old people and you didn't show up. You shouldn't watch so much TV.

A Oh I know.

B Is that a female impersonator?

A Of what?

A The most exciting thing is not-doing-it. If you fall in love with someone and never do it, it's much more exciting.

Love affairs get too involved, and they're not really worth it. But if, for some reason, you feel that they are, you should put in exactly as much time and energy as the other person. In other words, 'I'll pay you if you pay me.'

People have so many problems with love, always looking for someone to be their Via Veneto, their soufflé that can't fall. There should be a course in the first grade on love. There should be courses on beauty and love and sex. With love as the biggest course. And they should show the kids, I always think, how to make love and tell and show them once and for all how nothing it is. But they won't do that, because love and sex are business.

But then I think, maybe it works out just as well that nobody takes you out of the dark about it, because if you really knew the whole story, you wouldn't have anything to think about or fantasize about for the rest of your life, and you might go crazy, having nothing to think about, since life is getting longer, anyway, leaving so much time after puberty to have sex in.

I don't remember much about puberty. I probably missed most of it being sick in bed with my Charlie McCarthy doll, just like I missed *Snow White*. I didn't see *Snow White* until I was forty-five, when I went with Roman Polanski to see it at Lincoln Center. It was probably a good thing that I waited, because I can't imagine how it could ever be more exciting than it was then. Which gave me the idea that instead of telling kids very early about the mechanics and nothingness of sex, maybe it would be better to suddenly and very excitingly reveal the details to them when they're forty. You could be walking down the street with a friend who's just turned forty, spill the birds-and-the-bees beans, wait for the initial shock of learning what-goes-where to die down, and then patiently explain the rest. Then suddenly at forty their life would have new meaning. We should really stay babies for much longer than we do, now that we're living so much longer.

It's the long life-spans that are throwing all the old values and their applications out of whack. When people used to learn about sex at fifteen and die at thirty-five, they obviously were going to have fewer problems than people today who learn about sex at eight or so, I guess, and live to be eighty. That's a long time to play around with the same concept. The same boring concept.

Parents who really love their kids and want them to be bored and discontented for as small a percentage of their lifetimes as possible maybe should go back to not letting them date until as late as possible so they have something to look forward to for a longer time.

Sex is more exciting on the screen and between the pages than between the sheets anyway. Let the kids read about it and look forward to it, and then right before they're going to get the reality, break the news to them that they've already had the most exciting part, that it's behind them already.

Fantasy love is much better than reality love. Never doing it is very exciting. The most exciting attractions are between two opposites that never meet.

I love every 'lib' movement there is, because after the 'lib' the things that were always a mystique become understandable and boring, and then nobody has to feel left out if they're not part of what is happening. For instance, single people looking for husbands and wives used to feel left out because the image marriage had in the old days was so wonderful. Jane Wyatt and Robert Young. Nick and Nora Charles. Ethel and Fred Mertz. Dagwood and Blondie.

Being married looked so wonderful that life didn't seem livable if you weren't lucky enough to have a husband or wife. To the singles, marriage seemed beautiful, the trappings seemed wonderful, and the sex was always implied to be automatically great – no one could ever seem to find words to describe it because 'you had to be there' to know how good it was. It was almost like a conspiracy on the part of the married people not to let it out how it wasn't necessarily completely wonderful to be married and having sex; they could have taken a load off the single people's minds if they'd just been candid.

But it was always a fairly well-kept secret that if you were married to somebody you didn't have enough room in bed and might have to face bad breath in the morning.

There are so many songs about love. But I was thrilled the other day when somebody mailed me the lyrics to a song that was about how he didn't care about anything, and how he didn't care about me. It was very good. He managed to really convey the idea that he really didn't care.

I don't see anything wrong with being alone. It feels great to me. People make a big thing about personal love. It doesn't have to be such a big thing. The same for living – people make a big thing about that too. But personal living and personal loving are the two things the Eastern-type wise men *don't* think about.

I wonder if it's possible to have a love affair that lasts forever. If you're married for thirty years and you're 'cooking breakfast for the one you love' and he walks in, does his heart really skip a beat? I mean if it's just a regular morning. I guess it skips a beat over that breakfast and that's nice, too. It's nice to have a little breakfast made for you.

The biggest price you pay for love is that you have to have somebody around, you can't be on your own, which is always so much better. The biggest disadvantage, of course, is no room in bed. Even a pet cuts into your bed room.

I believe in long engagements. The longer, the better.

Love and sex can go together and sex and unlove can go together and love and unsex can go together. But personal love and personal sex is bad.

You can be just as faithful to a place or a thing as you can to a person. A place can really make your heart skip a beat, especially if you have to take a plane to get there.

Mom always said not to worry about love, but just to be sure to get married. But I always knew that I would never get married, because I don't want any children, I don't want them to have the same problems that I have. I don't think anybody deserves it.

I think a lot about the people who are supposed to not have any problems, who get married and live and die and it's all been wonderful. I don't know anybody like that. They always have some problem, even if it's only that the toilet doesn't flush.

My ideal wife would have a lot of bacon, bring it all home, and have a TV station besides.

I was always fascinated when I watched old war movies where the girls get married by proxy over the phone to husbands across the sea and they'd say, 'I hear you, my darling!' and I always thought how great it would be if they just stayed that way, they'd be so happy. I guess they wanted the monthly check, though.

I have a telephone mate. We've had an on-going relationship over the phone for six years. I live uptown and she lives downtown. It's a wonderful arrangement: we don't have to get each other's bad morning breath, yet we have wonderful breakfasts together every morning like every other happy couple. I'm uptown in the kitchen making myself peppermint tea and a dry, medium-to-dark English muffin with marmalade, and she's downtown waiting for the coffee shop to deliver a light coffee and a toasted roll with honey and butter – heavy on the light, honey, butter, and seeds. We while and talk away the sunny morning hours with the telephone nestled between head and shoulders and we can walk away or even hang up whenever we want to. We don't have to worry about kids, just about extension phones. We have an understanding. She married a staple-gun queen twelve years ago and has been more or less waiting for the annulment to come through ever since, although she tells people who ask that he died in a mudslide.

The symptom of love is when some of the chemicals inside you go bad. So there must be something in love because your chemicals do tell you something.

I tried and tried when I was younger to learn something about love, and since it wasn't taught in school I turned to the movies for some clues about what love is and what to do about it. In those days you did learn something about some kind of love from the movies, but it was nothing you could apply with any reasonable results. I mean, the other night I was watching on TV the 1961 version of *Back Street* with John Gavin and Susan Hayward and I was stunned the whole time because all they kept saying was how wonderful every precious moment they had together was, and so every precious moment was a testimonial to every precious moment.

But I always thought that movies could show you so much more about how it really is between people and therefore help all the people who don't understand to know what to do, what some of their options are.

What I was actually trying to do in my early movies was show how people can meet other people and what they can do and what they can say to each other. That was the whole idea: two people getting acquainted. And then when you saw it and you saw the sheer simplicity of it, you learned what it was all about. Those movies showed you how some people act and react with other people. They were like actual sociological 'For instances'. They were like documentaries, and if you thought it could apply to you, it was an example, and if it didn't apply to you, at least it was a documentary, it could apply to somebody you knew and it could clear up some questions you had about them.

In *Tub Girls*, for example, the girls had to take baths with people in tubs, and they learned how to take baths with other people. While we were doing *Tub Girls*. They met in a tub. And the girl would have to carry her tub to the next person she'd have to take a bath with, so she'd put her tub under her arm and carry her tub . . . We used a clear plastic tub.

I never particularly wanted to make simply sex movies. If I had wanted to make a real sex movie I would have filmed a flower giving birth to another flower. And the best love story is just two love-birds in a cage.

The best love is not-to-think-about-it love. Some people can have sex and really let their minds go blank and fill up with the sex; other people can never let their minds go blank and fill up with the sex, so while they're having the sex they're thinking, 'Can this really be me? Am I really doing this? This is very strange. Five minutes ago I wasn't doing this. In a little while I won't be doing it. What would Mom say? How did people ever think of doing this?' So the first type of person – the type that can let their minds go blank and fill up with sex and not-think-about-it – is better off. The other type has to find something else to relax with and get lost in. For me that something else is humor.

Funny people are the only people I ever get really interested in, because as soon as somebody isn't funny, they bore me. But if the big attraction for you is having somebody be funny, you run into a problem, because being funny is not being sexy, so in the end, near the moment of truth, you're not really attracted, you can't really 'do it.'

But I'd rather laugh in bed than do it. Get under the covers and crack jokes, I guess, is the best way. 'How am I doing?' 'Fine, that was very funny.' 'Wow, you were really funny tonight.'

If I went to a lady of the night, I'd probably pay her to tell me jokes.

Sometimes sex doesn't wear off. I've seen cases of couples where the sex for each other didn't wear off over the years.

Couples do become like each other when they're together for a long time, because you like the person and you pick up their mannerisms and their little good habits. And you eat the same food.

Everybody has a different idea of love. One girl I know said, 'I knew he loved me when he didn't come in my mouth.'

Over the years I've been more successful at dealing with love than with jealousy. I get jealousy attacks all the time. I think I may be one of the most jealous people in the world. My right hand is jealous if my left hand is painting a pretty picture. If my left leg is dancing a good step, my right leg gets jealous. The left side of my mouth is jealous when my right side is eating something good. I'm jealous at dinner that somebody else will think of something better to order than I did. I'm jealous of somebody's blurred Instamatics even when I have my own sharp Polaroids of the same scene. Basically, I go crazy when I can't have first choice on absolutely everything. A lot of times I do things I don't want to do at all, just because I'm on stand-by jealousy that somebody else will get to do it instead. As a matter of fact, I'm always trying to buy things and people just because I'm so jealous somebody else might buy them and they might turn out to be good after all. That's one of the stories of my life. And the few times in my life when I've gone on television, I've been so jealous of the host on the show that I haven't been able to talk. As soon as the TV cameras turn on, all I can think is, 'I want my own show . . . I want my own show.'

I get very nervous when I think someone is falling in love with me. Every time I have a 'romance' I'm so nervous I bring the whole office with me. That's usually about five or six people. They all come to pick me up and then we go to pick her up. Love me, love my office.

Everybody winds up kissing the wrong person goodnight. One of my ways of thanking the office for coming with me to chaperone is to make myself available to chaperone their dates. One or two of them like to take advantage of that service, because one or two of them are a little like me, they don't want anything to happen. When *I'm* there, they tell me, nothing happens. I make nothing happen. Wherever I go. I can tell when one of them is glad to see me walk in the door, because something's happening and they can't wait for me to make nothing happen. Especially when they're stranded in Italy, because you know how the Italians like to make something happen. I'm the obvious antidote.

People should fall in love with their eyes closed. Just close your eyes. Don't look.

Some people I know spend a lot of time trying to dream up new seductions. I used to think that only the people who didn't work had time to think about those kinds of things but then I realized that most people are using somebody else's time to dream up their new seductions. Most of the people in offices are actually getting paid while they day-dream up their new seductions.

I believe in low lights and trick mirrors. A person is entitled to the lighting they need. Plus, if you learn about sex when you're forty, as suggested earlier, you'd better believe in low lights and trick mirrors.

Love can be bought and sold. One of the older superstars used to cry every time somebody she loved kicked her out of his loft, and I used to tell her, 'Don't worry. You're going to be very famous someday and you'll be able to buy him.' It worked out just that way and she's very happy now.

Brigitte Bardot was one of the first women to be really modern and treat men like love objects, buying them and discarding them. I like that.

The most fashionable girls around town now are the girls of the night. They wear the most fashionable clothes. They were always behind the times, looking old-fashioned, but now they're the first ones on the street with the new clothes. They wised up. More intelligent girls are girls of the night now, too. More liberated. But they all still use those ugly shoulder pocketbooks.

Sex-and-nostalgia is funny to think about. I was walking on the West Side in the Forties, around the honky tonks and I was looking at the 8 x 10 glossies of girls that they put out front. One window-case display had a very 50s look but the pictures weren't yellow with age or anything, so I couldn't tell if those exact girls were inside right then or if that was an old picture left over and the girls inside, instead of being Mamie Van Doren types, were tired ex-hippies. I didn't know. The establishment might have

52

been catering to a crowd who were nostalgic for all the girls they'd tried to pick up in the 50s.

With everything changing so fast, you don't have a chance of finding your fantasy image intact by the time you're ready for it. What about all the little boys who used to have fantasies about girls in beautiful lace bras and silk slips? They don't have a chance of finding what they'd always looked forward to, unless the girl had just made a trip to the local thrift shop, and that's worse than nothing.

Fantasy and clothes go together a lot, but the times and *mores* have thrown that off, too. When clothes-makers were making good clothes out of good materials, an ordinary guy who bought a suit or a shirt without giving too much thought to anything except 'Does it fit?' would be likely to come away with a nice-looking suit with good detailing out of a nice piece of material.

But then labor got expensive and the manufacturers began giving a little less good workmanship for the money every year, and nobody really complained, so they pushed – and they're still pushing to the limit – how little can they give before people will say, 'Is this a shirt?' The moderate-priced clothes-makers really are giving people junk these days. On top of the awful way the clothes are made – long stitches, no linings, no darts, no finished seams – they're made out of synthetics that look awful from the first to the last wearing. (The only good synthetic is nylon, I think.)

No, a person has to be very careful about what he's buying these days or else he'll wind up buying junk. And paying a lot for it too. So this means that *if you see a well-dressed person today, you know that they've thought a lot about their clothes and how they look.* And then that ruins it because you shouldn't really be thinking about how you look so much. The same applies to girls but not as much – they can care a little more about themselves without being unattractively self-interested, because they're naturally prettier. But a man caring about how he looks is usually trying very hard to be attractive, and that's very unattractive in a man.

So today, if you see a person who looks like your teenage fantasy walking down the street, it's probably not your fantasy, but someone who had the same fantasy as you and decided instead of getting it or being it, to *look like it*, and so he went to the store and bought the look that you both like. So forget it.

Just think about all the James Deans and what it means.

Truman Capote told me once that certain kinds of sex are total, complete manifestations of nostalgia, and I think that's true. Other kinds of sex have nostalgia in varying degrees, from a little to a lot, but I think it's safe to say that most sex involves some form of nostalgia for something.

Sex is a nostalgia for when you used to want it, sometimes.

Sex is nostalgia for sex.

Some people think violence is sexy, but I could never see that.

'Love' used to have a good number always in Mom's dream book. When I was little Mom used to play the numbers and I remember she used to have a dream book and she'd look up her dream and the book would tell her whether it was a good dream or not, and there were numbers after it which she played. And 'Love' dreams always had a good number.

When you want to be like something, it means you really love it. When you want to be like a rock, you really love that rock. I love plastic idols.

People with pretty smiles fascinate me. You have to wonder what makes them smile so pretty.

People look the most kissable when they're not wearing makeup. Marilyn's lips weren't kissable, but they were very photographable.

54

One of my movies, *Women in Revolt*, was originally entitled *Sex*, I can't now remember why we changed its name. The three female leads were three female impersonators – Candy Darling, Jackie Curtis, and Holly Woodlawn. They played women in varying degrees and various stages of 'liberation'.

Among other things, drag queens are living testimony to the way women used to want to be, the way some people still want them to be, and the way some women still actually want to be. Drags are ambulatory archives of ideal moviestar womanhood. They perform a documentary service, usually consecrating their lives to keeping the glittering alternative alive and available for (not-too-close) inspection.

To get a private room in a hospital you used to have to be very rich but now you can get one if you're a drag queen. If you're a drag queen they want to isolate you from the other patients, but maybe they have enough for a ward now.

I'm fascinated by boys who spend their lives trying to be complete girls, because they have to work so hard – double-time – getting rid of all the tell-tale male signs and drawing in all the female signs. I'm not saying it's the right thing to do, I'm not saying it's a good idea, I'm not saying it's not self-defeating and self-destructive, and I'm not saying it's not possibly the single most absurd thing a man can do with his life. What I'm saying is, it is very hard work. You can't take that away from them. It's hard work to look like the complete opposite of what nature made you and then to be an imitation woman of what was only a fantasy woman in the first place. When they took the movie stars and stuck them in the kitchen, they weren't stars any more – they were just like you and me. Drag queens are reminders that some stars still aren't just like you and me.

For a while we were casting a lot of drag queens in our movies because the real girls we knew couldn't seem to get excited about anything, and the drag queens could get excited about anything. But lately the girls seem to be getting their energy back, so we've been using real ones a lot again.

55

In *Women in Revolt*, Jackie Curtis ad-libbed one of the best lines
of disillusionment with sex when he-as-she, portraying a virgin
schoolteacher from Bayonne, New Jersey, was forced to give oral
gratification – a blow-job – to Mr America. After gagging and
somehow finishing up, poor Jackie can't figure out if she's had sex
or not – 'This can't be what millions of girls commit suicide over
when their boy-friends leave them . . .' Jackie was acting out the
puzzled thoughts so many people have when they realize that sex
is hard work just like everything else.

People's fantasies are what give them problems. If you didn't have
fantasies you wouldn't have problems because you'd just take
whatever was there. But then you wouldn't have romance,
because romance is finding your fantasy in people who don't have
it. A friend of mine always says, 'Women love me for the man I'm
not.'

It's very easy to make *faux pas* when you're talking to a person
who's in love, because they're more sensitive about everything. I
remember once I was at a dinner party and I was talking to a
couple who looked so happy together and I said, 'You are the
happiest-looking couple I've ever seen.' That was okay and then I
went that little bit further to score my nightly *faux pas*. 'It must
have been like a storybook dream love story. I just know you were
childhood sweethearts.' And at that point their faces fell and they
turned away and avoided me for the rest of the evening. I found
out later that they had deserted their husbands and wives and
families to go after each other.

So you really have to watch what you say to people about their
love lives. When people are in love all their problems are in
strange proportions and it's hard to know when you're saying the
wrong thing.

To think about the love problems of people you know is really
strange, because their love problems are so different from their
life problems.

A drag queen I know is waiting for a real man to fall in love with
him/her.

I always run into strong women who are looking for weak men to dominate them.

I don't know anybody who doesn't have a fantasy. Everybody must have a fantasy.

A movie producer friend of mine hit on something when he said, 'Frigid people can really make out.' He's right: they really can and they really do.

4 Beauty

B Does she wear someone's clothes or does she just get them herself?

A Oh no no no no. She wears her husband's clothes – she goes to the same tailor. That's what they fight about.

I've never met a person I couldn't call a beauty.

Every person has beauty at some point in their lifetime. Usually in different degrees. Sometimes they have the looks when they're a baby and they don't have it when they're grown up, but then they could get it back again when they're older. Or they might be fat but have a beautiful face. Or have bow-legs but a beautiful body. Or be the number one female beauty and have no tits. Or be the number one male beauty and have a small you-know-what.

Some people think it's easier for beauties, but actually it can work out a lot of different ways. If you're beautiful you might have a pea-brain. If you're not beautiful you might not have a pea-brain, so it depends on the pea-brain and the beauty. The size of the beauty. And the pea-brain.

I always hear myself saying, 'She's a beauty!' or 'He's a beauty!' or 'What a beauty!' but I never know what I'm talking about. I honestly don't know what beauty is, not to speak of what 'a' beauty is. So that leaves me in a strange position, because I'm noted for how much I talk about 'this one's a beauty' and 'that one's a beauty'. For a year once it was in all the magazines that my next movie was going to be *The Beauties*. The publicity for it was great, but then I could never decide who should be in it. If everybody's not a beauty, then nobody is, so I didn't want to imply that the kids in *The Beauties* were beauties but the kids in my other movies weren't so I had to back out on the basis of the title. It was all wrong.

I really don't care that much about 'Beauties'. What I really like are Talkers. To me, good talkers are beautiful because good talk is what I love. The word itself shows why I like Talkers better than Beauties, why I tape more than I film. It's not 'talkies'. Talkers are *doing* something. Beauties are *being* something. Which isn't necessarily bad, it's just that I don't know what it is they're being. It's more fun to be with people who are doing things.

When I did my self-portrait, I left all the pimples out because you always should. Pimples are a temporary condition and they don't have anything to do with what you really look like. Always omit the blemishes – they're not part of the good picture you want.

When a person is the beauty of their day, and their looks are really in style, and then the times change and tastes change, and ten years go by, if they keep exactly their same look and don't change anything and if they take care of themselves, they'll still be a beauty.

Schrafft's restaurants were the beauties of their day, and then they tried to keep up with the times and they modified and modified until they lost all their charm and were bought by a big company. But if they could just have kept their same look and style, and held on through the lean years when they weren't in style, today they'd be the best thing around. You have to hang on in periods when your style isn't popular, because if it's good, it'll come back, and you'll be a recognized beauty once again.

Some kind of beauty dwarfs you and makes you feel like an ant next to it. I was once in Mussolini Stadium with all the statues and they were so much bigger than life and I felt just like an ant. I was painting a beauty this afternoon and my paint caught a little bug. I tried to get the paint off the bug and I kept trying until I killed the bug on the beauty's lip. So there was this bug, that could have been a beauty, left on somebody's lip. That's the way I felt in Mussolini Stadium. Like a bug.

Beauties in photographs are different from beauties in person. It must be hard to be a model, because you'd want to be like the photograph of you, and you can't ever look that way. And so you start to copy the photograph. Photographs usually bring in another half-dimension. (Movies bring in another whole dimension. That screen magnetism is something secret – if you could only figure out what it is and how to make it, you'd have a really good product to sell. But you can't even tell if someone has it until you actually see them up there on the screen. You have to give screen tests to find out.)

Very few Beauties are Talkers, but there are a few.
  Beauty sleep.   Sleeping beauty.
  Beauty problems.   Problem beauties.

Even beauties can be unattractive. If you catch a beauty in the wrong light at the right time, forget it.
  I believe in low lights and trick mirrors.
  I believe in plastic surgery.

At one time the way my nose looked really bothered me – it's always red – and I decided that I wanted to have it sanded. Even the people in my family called me 'Andy the Red-Nosed Warhola'. I went to see the doctor and I think he thought he'd humor me, so he sanded it, and when I walked out of St Luke's Hospital I was the same underneath, but I had a bandage on.

They don't put you to sleep but they spray frozen stuff all over your face from a spray can. Then they take a sandpaperer and spin it around all over your face. It's very painful afterwards. You stay in for two weeks waiting for the scab to fall off. I did all that and it actually made my pores bigger. I was really disappointed.

I had another skin problem, too – I lost all my pigment when I was eight years old. Another name people used to call me was 'Spot'. This is how I think I lost my pigment: I saw a girl walking down the street and she was two-toned and I was so fascinated I kept following her. Within two months I was two-toned myself. And I hadn't even known the girl – she was just somebody I saw on the street. I asked a medical student if he thought I caught it just by looking at her. He didn't say anything.

About twenty years ago I went to Georgette Klinger's Skin Clinic and Georgette turned me down. It was before she had a men's department and she discriminated against me.

If people want to spend their whole lives creaming and tweezing and brushing and tilting and gluing, that's really okay too, because it gives them something to do.

Sometimes people having nervous breakdown problems can look very beautiful because they have that fragile something to the way they move or walk. They put out a mood that makes them more beautiful.

People tell me that some beauties lose their looks in bed when they don't do the bed things they're supposed to. I don't believe those things.

When you're interested in somebody, and you think they might be interested in you, you should point out all your beauty problems and defects right away, rather than take a chance they won't notice them. Maybe, say, you have a permanent beauty problem you can't change, such as too-short legs. Just say it. 'My legs, as you've probably noticed, are much too short in proportion to the rest of my body.' Why give the other person the satisfaction of discovering it for themselves? Once it's out in the open, at least you know it will never become an issue later on in the relationship, and if it does, you can always say, 'Well I told you that in the beginning.'

On the other hand, say you have a purely temporary beauty problem – a new pimple, lackluster hair, no-sleep eyes, five extra pounds around the middle. Still, whatever it is, you should point it out. If you don't point it out and say, 'My hair is really dull this time of the month, I'm probably getting my friend,' or 'I put on five pounds eating Russell Stover chocolates over Christmas, but I'm taking it off right away' – if you don't point out these things they might think that your temporary beauty problem is a permanent beauty problem. Why should they think otherwise if you've just met them? Remember, they've never seen you before in their life. So it's up to you to set them straight and get them to use their imagination about what your hair must look like when it's shiny, and what your body must look like when it's not over-weight, and what your dress would look like without the grease spot on it. Even explain that you have much better clothes hanging in your closet than the ones you're wearing. If they really do like you for yourself, they'll be willing to use their imagination

64

to think of what you must look like without your temporary beauty problem.

If you're naturally pale, you should put on a lot of blush-on to compensate. But if you've got a big nose, just play it up, and if you have a pimple, put on the pimple cream in a way that will make it really stand out – 'There! I use pimple cream!' There's a difference.

I always think that when people turn around to look at somebody on the street it's probably that they smell an odor from them, and that's what makes them turn around and on.

Diana Vreeland, the editor of *Vogue* for ten years, is one of the most beautiful women in the world because she's not afraid of other people, she does what she wants. Truman Capote brought up something else about her – she's very very clean, and that makes her more beautiful. Maybe it's even the basis of her beauty.

Being clean is so important. Well-groomed people are the real beauties. It doesn't matter what they're wearing or who they're with or how much their jewelry costs or how much their clothes cost or how perfect their makeup is: if they're not clean, they're not beautiful. The most plain or unfashionable person in the world can still be beautiful if they're very well-groomed.

During the 60s a lot of people I knew seemed to think that underarm smell was attractive. They never seemed to be wearing anything washable. Everything always had to be dry-cleaned – the satins, the sewn-on mirrors, the velvets – the problem was that it never was dry-cleaned. And then it got worse when everybody was wearing suedes and leathers, and those *really* never got cleaned. I admit to having worn suede and leather pants myself for a while, but you just never feel clean, and it's degenerate, anyway, to wear animal skins unless it's to keep yourself warm. I'll never understand why they haven't invented something yet that's as warm as fur. So I went back to bluejeans after that degenerate period. Very happily. Bluejeans wind up being the cleanest thing you can wear, because it's just their nature to be washed a lot. And they're so American in essence.

Beauty really has to do with the way a person carries it off. When you see 'beauty', it has to do with the place, with what they're wearing, what they're standing next to, what closet they're coming down the stairs from.

Jewelry doesn't make a person more beautiful, but it makes a person *feel* more beautiful. If you draped a beautiful person in jewels and beautiful clothes and put them in a beautiful house with beautiful furniture and beautiful paintings, they wouldn't be more beautiful, they'd be the same, but they would *think* they were more beautiful. However, if you took a beautiful person and put them in rags, they'd be ugly. You can always make a person less beautiful.

Beauty in danger becomes more beautiful, but beauty in dirt becomes ugly.

What makes a painting beautiful is the way the paint's put on, but I don't understand how women put on makeup. It gets on your lips, and it's so heavy. Lipstick and makeup and powder and shadow creams. And jewelry. It's all so heavy.

Children are always beautiful. Every kid, up to, say, eight years old always looks good. Even if the kid wears glasses it still looks good. They always have the perfect nose. I've never seen an unattractive baby. Small features and nice skin. This also applies to animals – I've never seen a bad-looking animal. Babies by being beautiful are protected because people want less to hurt them. This applies also to all animals.

Beauty doesn't have anything to do with sex. Beauty has to do with beauty and sex has to do with sex.

If a person isn't generally considered beautiful, they can still be a success if they have a few jokes in their pockets. And a lot of pockets.

Beautiful people are sometimes more prone to keep you waiting than plain people are, because there's a big time differential between beautiful and plain. Also, beauties know that most people will wait for them, so they're not panicked when they're late, so they get even later. But by the time they arrive, they've usually gotten to feel guilty, so then to make up for being late they get really sweet, and being really sweet makes them more beautiful. That's a classic syndrome.

I'm always trying to figure out whether if a woman is funny, she can still be beautiful. There are some very attractive comediennes, but if you had to choose between calling them beautiful and calling them funny, you'd call them funny. Sometimes I think that *extreme* beauty must be absolutely humorless. But then I think of Marilyn Monroe and she had the best funny lines. She might have been a lot of fun if she'd found the right comedy niche. We might be laughing at skits on 'The Marilyn Monroe Show' today.

Someone once asked me to state once and for all the most beautiful person I'd ever met. Well, the only people I can ever pick out as unequivocal beauties are from the movies, and then when you meet them, they're not really beauties either, so your standards don't even really exist. In life, the movie stars can't even come up to the standards they set on film.

Some of the very beautiful film stars of the past decades have aged beautifully and some have aged not-so-beautifully, and sometimes you see two stars together today who were once beautiful together in the same movie a long time ago, and now one of them looks and acts like an old woman and the other still looks and acts like a girl. But all of that doesn't matter very much, I think, because history will remember each person only for their beautiful moments on film – the rest is off-the-record.

A good plain look is my favorite look. If I didn't want to look so 'bad', I would want to look 'plain'. That would be my next choice.

I always think about what it means to wear eyeglasses. When you get used to glasses you don't know how far you could really see. I think about all the people before eyeglasses were invented. It must have been weird because everyone was seeing in different ways according to how bad their eyes were. Now, eyeglasses standardize everyone's vision to 20-20. That's an example of everyone becoming more alike. Everyone could be seeing at different levels if it weren't for glasses.

In some circles where very heavy people think they have very heavy brains, words like 'charming' and 'clever' and 'pretty' are all put-downs; all the lighter things in life, which are the most important things, are put down.

Weight isn't important the way the magazines make you think it is. I know a girl who just looks at her face in the medicine cabinet mirror and never looks below her shoulders, and she's four or five hundred pounds but she doesn't see all that, she just sees a beautiful face and therefore she thinks she's a beauty. And therefore I think she's a beauty, too, because I usually accept people on the basis of their self-images, because their self-images have more to do with the way they think than their objective-images do. Maybe she's six hundred pounds, who knows. If she doesn't care, I don't.

But if you do watch your weight, try the Andy Warhol New York City Diet: when I order in a restaurant, I order everything I don't want, so I have a lot to play around with while everyone else eats. Then, no matter how chic the restaurant is, I insist that the waiter wrap the entire plate up like a to-go order, and after we leave the restaurant I find a little corner outside in the street to leave the plate in, because there are so many people in New York who live in the streets, with everything they own in shopping bags.

So I lose weight and stay trim, and I think that maybe one of those people will find a Grenouille dinner on the window ledge. But then, you never know, maybe they wouldn't like what I ordered as much as I didn't like it, and maybe they'd turn up their noses and look through the garbage for some half-eaten rye bread. You just never know with people. You just never know what they'll like, what you should do for them.

So that's the Andy Warhol New York City Diet.

I know good cooks who'll spend days finding fresh garlic and fresh basil and fresh tarragon, etc., and then use canned tomatoes for the sauce, saying it doesn't matter. But I know it does matter.

Whenever people and civilizations get degenerate and materialistic, they always point at their outward beauty and riches and say that if what they were doing was bad, they wouldn't be doing so well, being so rich and beautiful. People in the Bible did that when they worshipped the Golden Calf, for example, and then the Greeks when they worshiped the human body. But beauty and riches couldn't have anything to do with how good you are, because think of all the beauties who get cancer. And a lot of murderers are good-looking, so that settles it.

Some people, even intelligent people, say that violence can be beautiful. I can't understand that, because beautiful is some moments, and for me those moments are never violent.

A new idea.
A new look.
A new sex.
A new pair of underwear.

There should be a lot of new girls in town, and there always are.

The red lobster's beauty only comes out when it's dropped into the boiling water . . . and nature changes things and carbon is turned into diamonds and dirt is gold . . . and wearing a ring in your nose is gorgeous.

I can never get over when you're on the beach how beautiful the sand looks and the water washes it away and straightens it up and the trees and the grass all look great. I think having land and not ruining it is the most beautiful art that anybody could ever want to own.

The most beautiful thing in Tokyo is McDonald's.

The most beautiful thing in Stockholm is McDonald's.

The most beautiful thing in Florence is McDonald's.

69

Peking and Moscow don't have anything beautiful yet.

America is really The Beautiful. But it would be more beautiful if everybody had enough money to live.

Beautiful jails for Beautiful People.

Everybody's sense of beauty is different from everybody else's. When I see people dressed in hideous clothes that look all wrong on them, I try to imagine the moment when they were buying them and thought, 'This is great. I like it. I'll take it.' You can't imagine what went off in their heads to make them buy those maroon polyester waffle-iron pants or that acrylic halter top that has 'Miami' written in glitter. You wonder what they rejected as *not* beautiful – an acrylic halter top that had 'Chicago'?

You can never predict what little things in the way somebody looks or talks or acts will set off peculiar emotional reactions in other people. For instance, the other night I was with a lady who suddenly got very intense about a person we both knew and she started to tear apart his looks – his weak arms, his pimply face, his bad posture, his thick eyebrows, his big nose, his bad clothes, and I didn't know what to say because I didn't see why she would be seen with me if she wouldn't be seen with him. After all, I have weak arms, I have pimples, but she didn't seem to notice my problems. I think that some little thing can set off reactions in people, and you don't know what it is in their past that's making them like or not like somebody so much and therefore like or not like everything about them.

Sometimes something can look beautiful just because it's different in some way from the other things around it. One red petunia in a window box will look very beautiful if all the rest of them are white, and vice-versa.

When you're in Sweden and you see beautiful person after beautiful person after beautiful person and you finally don't even turn around to look because you know the next person you see will be just as beautiful as the one you didn't bother to turn around to look at – in a place like that you can get so bored that when you see a person who's not beautiful, they look very beautiful to you because they break the beautiful monotony.

There are three things that always look very beautiful to me: my same good pair of old shoes that don't hurt, my own bedroom, and US Customs on the way back home.

5 Fame

B   What did those record people want?

A   They want me to cut a record. They'll make my voice sound like it's singing.

A   I love your *Daily News* commercial on television. I've seen it fifteen times.

Some company recently was interested in buying my 'aura'. They didn't want my product. They kept saying, 'We want your aura.' I never figured out what they wanted. But they were willing to pay a lot for it. So then I thought that if somebody was willing to pay that much for my it, I should try to figure out what it is.

I think 'aura' is something that only somebody else can see, and they only see as much of it as they want to. It's all in the other person's eyes. You can only see an aura on people you don't know very well or don't know at all. I was having dinner the other night with everybody from my office. The kids at the office treat me like dirt, because they know me and they see me every day. But then there was this nice friend that somebody had brought along who had never met me, and this kid could hardly believe that he was having dinner with me! Everybody else was seeing me, but he was seeing my 'aura'.

When you just see somebody on the street, they can really have an aura. But then when they open their mouth, there goes the aura. 'Aura' must be until you open your mouth.

The people who have the best fame are those who have their name on stores. The people with very big stores named after them are the ones I'm really jealous of. Like Marshall Field.

But being famous isn't all that important. If I weren't famous, I wouldn't have been shot for being Andy Warhol. Maybe I would have been shot for being in the Army. Or maybe I would be a fat schoolteacher. How do you ever know?

A good reason to be famous, though, is so you can read all the big magazines and know everybody in all the stories. Page after page it's just all people you've met. I love that kind of reading experience and that's the best reason to be famous.

I'm confused about who the news belongs to. I always have it in my head that if your name's in the news, then the news should be paying you. Because it's *your news* and they're taking it and selling it as their product. But then they always say that they're helping you, and that's true too, but still, if people didn't give the news their news, and if everybody kept their news to themselves, the news wouldn't have any news. So I guess you should pay each other. But I haven't figured it out fully yet.

The worst, most cruel review of me that I ever read was the *Time* magazine review of me getting shot.

I've found that almost all interviews are preordained. They know what they want to write about you and they know what they think about you before they ever talk to you, so they're just looking for words and details from here and there to back up what they've already decided they're going to say. If you go into an interview blind, there is absolutely no way of guessing what kind of article the person you're talking to is going to write. The nicest, laughingest people can write the meanest articles, and the people you think are hating you can write the funniest, nicest articles. It's harder to tell with journalists than with politicians.

When somebody writes a really mean article, I always just let it go by because who are you to say it isn't the truth?

People used to say that I tried to 'put on' the media when I would give one autobiography to one newspaper and another autobiography to another newspaper. I used to like to give different information to different magazines because it was like putting a tracer on where people get their information. That way I could always tell when I met people what newspapers and magazines they were reading by the things they would tell me I had said. Sometimes funny pieces of information come back to you years and years later when an interviewer says, 'You once said that Lefrak City was the most beautiful place in the world', and then you know that they've read what you once told *Architectural Forum*.

The right story in the right place can really put you up-there for months or even years. I lived next to a Gristedes grocery for twelve years, and every day I would go in and drift around the aisles, picking out what I wanted – that's a ritual I really enjoy. For twelve years I did this just about every day. Then one afternoon the New York *Post* ran a color picture of Monique Van Vooren and Rudolf Nureyev and me on the front page, and when I next went into the store all the stockboys started yelling 'Here he is!' and 'I told you it was him!' I didn't want to go back there ever again. Then after my picture was in *Time*, I couldn't take my dog to the park for a week because people were pointing at me.

Up until a year ago I was a real nobody in Italy. I was somebody – maybe – in Germany and England – which is why I no longer go to those countries – but in Italy they couldn't even spell my name. Then *L'Uomo Vogue* found out how to spell my name from a superstar of ours who started going with one of their photographers – pillow talk I guess – but anyway, he leaked the correct spelling of my name to *L'Uomo* and then he leaked the titles of my movies and photos of my paintings and now I'm a fad in Italy. In fact, I was just in a very small town called Boissano, on the wrong side of the Riviera, and I was having an aperitif on the terrace of the local news-stand and a young fellow, a high school student, came up to me and said, 'Hi, Andy, how's Holly Woodlawn doing?' I was shocked. He knew about five words of English and four of them were FLESH, TRASH, HEAT, and DALLESANDRO, which maybe doesn't count because it's Italian.

I'm always interested in talk-show hosts. A person I know told me he can look at people who do interviews on television and know where they're from, what kind of schools they went to, what religion they are, just by seeing what kind of guests they have on their show and by hearing what kind of questions they ask their guests. I'd love to be able to know everything about a person from watching them on television – to be able to tell *what their problem is*. Can you imagine watching a talk show and knowing immediately things like—

'This one's problem is HE WANTS TO BE A BEAUTY.'
'This one's problem is HE HATES RICH PEOPLE.'
'This one's problem is HE CAN'T GET IT UP.'
'That one's problem is HE WANTS TO BE MISERABLE.'
'This one's problem is HE WANTS TO BE INTELLIGENT.'

And maybe you'd also be able to figure out—

'Why Dinah Shore DOESN'T HAVE A PROBLEM.'

I would also be thrilled to be able to know what color eyes a person has just from looking at them, because color TV still can't help you too much there.

Certain people have TV magic: they fall completely apart off-camera but they are completely together on-camera. They shake and sweat before they go on, they shake and sweat during commercials, they shake and sweat when it's all over; but while the camera is filming them, they're poised and confident-looking. The camera turns them on and off.

I never fall apart because I never fall together. I just sit there saying 'I'm going to faint. I'm going to faint. I know I'm going to faint. Have I fainted yet? I'm going to faint.' When I'm on television I can't think about anything they're going to ask me, I can't think about anything that's going to come out of my mouth – all I can think is, 'Is this a live show? It is? Well then forget it, I'm going to faint. I'm waiting for a faint.' That's my live television appearance stream-of-consciousness. Taped is different.

And I always thought that talk-show hosts and other television personalities could never know what it's like to feel that nervous, but then I realized that some of them might actually have a variation of the same problem – maybe every minute they're thinking 'I'm going to blow it, I'm going to blow it . . . there goes the summer house in East Hampton . . . there goes the Park Avenue co-op . . . there goes the sauna . . .' The difference is that while they're thinking their version of 'I'm going to faint',

78

they can somehow – through their TV magic – keep pulling out the lines and stuff they have stored somewhere.

There are some people who just begin performing when they're 'on'. 'On' is different things to different people. I was watching a young actor accepting his Emmy on television and he went up there on the stage, and he turned right on, he went right into his acting to say, 'I want to say thanks, thanks to my wife—' and he was doing a 'meaningful moment' scene. He was having a ball. I started thinking what a big fantastic moment getting an award like that must be for a person who can only turn 'on' when he's in front of people. If that's what turns him on, when he gets that chance, he has to be up there feeling *fine*, thinking, 'I can do anything, anything, ANYTHING!'

So I guess everybody has their own time and place when they turn themselves on.

Where do I turn on?

I turn on when I turn off and go to bed. That's my big moment that I'm always waiting for.

'Good performers', I think, are all-inclusive recorders, because they can mimic emotions as well as speech and looks and atmosphere – they're more inclusive than tape recordings or videotapes or novels. Good performers can somehow record complete experiences and people and situations and then pull out these recordings when they need them. They can repeat a line exactly the way it should sound and look exactly the way they should look when they repeat it because they've seen the scene before somewhere and they've shelved it away. So they know what the lines should be and the way the lines should come out of them. Or stay in them.

I can only understand really amateur performers or really bad performers, because whatever they do never really comes off, so therefore it can't be phoney. But I can never understand really good, professional performers.

Every professional performer I've ever seen always does exactly the same thing at exactly the same moment in every show they do. They know when the audience is going to laugh and when it's going to get really interested. What I like are things that are different every time. That's why I like amateur performers and bad performers – you can never tell what they'll do next.

Jackie Curtis used to write plays and stage them on Second Avenue, and the play would change every night – the lines and even the plot. Only the name of the play would stay the same. If two people saw the show on different nights and started talking about it to each other, they found out that nothing was the same in the two shows. The runs of these plays were 'evolutionary', as the play kept changing all the time.

I know that 'professional' is fast, and it's good, and people are on time, and they show up, and they do it right, and they're on key, and they do their numbers, and there are no problems. You watch them perform and they look so natural you just can't believe they're not ad-libbing – it looks like the funny line just occurred to them at the moment they said it. But then you go to see them the next night and the same funny line is just occurring to them all over again.

If I ever have to cast an acting role, I want the wrong person for the part. I can never visualize the right person in a part. The right person for the right part would be too much. Besides, no person is ever completely right for any part, because a part is a role is never real, so if you can't get someone who's perfectly right, it's more satisfying to get someone who's perfectly wrong. Then you know you've really got something.

The wrong people always look so right to me. And when you've got a lot of people and they're all 'good', it's hard to make distinctions, the easiest thing is to pick the really bad person. And I always go after the easiest thing, because if it's the easiest, for me it's usually the best.

I was doing a commercial the other day for some sound equipment, and I could have pretended to say all the words they gave me that I would never say that way, but I just couldn't do it.

When I played an airport person in a movie with Elizabeth

Taylor the lines they gave me were something like 'Let's go. I have an important date', but it kept coming out of my mouth, 'Come on, girls.' But in Italy they dub everything in afterwards, so no matter what you don't say, you say it anyway.

I did an airline commercial once with Sonny Liston – 'If you've got it, flaunt it!' I liked saying that, but then later they dubbed my voice, although they didn't dub his.

Some people say that you're only impressed with somebody famous if you've known about them since you were little or for a long time before you met them. They say that if you've never heard of an individual and you meet them, and then afterwards somebody comes over and tells you that you've just met the richest, most famous person in, say, Germany, you would not be so impressed at having met them, because you yourself had never put any of your own time into thinking about how famous they are. However, *I feel just the opposite*: I'm not impressed with all these funny people that everybody thinks are famous, because I always feel they're the easiest to meet. What I'm most impressed with is when I meet somebody I thought I could never meet – that I'd never dream I'd be talking to some day. People like Kate Smith, Lassie, Paloma Picasso's mother, Nixon, Mamie Eisenhower, Tab Hunter, Charlie Chaplin.

When I was little I used to listen to The Singing Lady on the radio all the time while I was in bed coloring. Then in 1972 I was at a party in New York and I was introduced to a woman and they said, 'She used to be The Singing Lady on the radio.' I was just incredulous. I could hardly believe that I was really meeting her, because I never dreamed that I would ever meet her. I'd just assumed that there was no chance at all. When you meet someone you never dreamed you'd meet, you're taken by surprise, so you haven't made up any fantansies and you're not let down.

Some people spend their whole lives thinking about one particular famous person. They pick one person who's famous, and they dwell on him or her. They devote almost their entire consciousness to thinking about this person they've never even met, or maybe met once. If you ask any famous person about the kind of mail they get, you'll find that almost every one of them has at least one person who's obsessed with them and writes constantly. It feels so strange to think that someone is spending their whole time thinking about you.

Nutty people are always writing me. I always think I must be on some nutty mailing list.

I always worry that when nutty people do something, they'll do the same thing again a few years later without ever remembering that they've done it before – and they'll think it's a whole new thing they're doing. I was shot in 1968, so that was the 1968 version. But then I have to think, 'Will someone want to do a 1970s remake of shooting me?' So that's another kind of fan.

In the early days of film, fans used to idolize a *whole* star – they would take one star and love everything about that star. Today there are different fan levels. Now fans only idolize *parts* of the stars. Today people can idolize a star in one area and forget about him in another. A big rock star might sell millions and millions of records, but then if he makes a bad movie, and when the word gets around that it's bad, forget it.

New categories of people are now being put up there as stars. The sports people are making themselves into great new stars. (Something I think about when I'm watching things like Olympic meets is 'When will a person not break a record?' If somebody runs at 2.2, does that mean that people will next be able to do it at 2.1 and 2.0 and 1.9 and so on until they can do it in 0.0? So at what point will they not break a record? Will they have to change the time or change the record?)

Nowadays if you're a crook you're still considered up-there. You can write books, go on TV, give interviews – you're a big celebrity and nobody even looks down on you because you're a crook. You're still really up-there. This is because more than anything people just want stars.

Good b.o. means good 'box office'. You can smell it from a mile away. The more you spell it out, the bigger the smell, and the bigger the smell, the more b.o. you get.

Working for a lot of money can throw your self-image off. When I used to do shoe drawings for the magazines I would get a certain amount for each shoe, so then I would count up my shoes to figure out how much I was going to get. I lived by the number of shoe drawings – when I counted them I knew how much money I had.

Models can sometimes be very rude. Because they get paid by the hour and put in their eight-hour day, when they go home they think they should still be getting paid. Movie stars get millions of dollars for nothing, so when someone asks them to do something for nothing, they go crazy – they think that if they're going to talk to somebody at the grocery store they should get fifty dollars an hour.

So you should always have a product that's not just 'you'. An actress should count up her plays and movies and a model should count up her photographs and a writer should count up his words and an artist should count up his pictures so you always know exactly what you're worth, and you don't get stuck thinking your product is you and your fame, and your aura.

6 Work

B Hospitals are unbelievable.
A When I was dying I had to write my name on a check.

fired – so the whole scene is much funnier than the real scene where everything went right, and the girl who didn't jump is the star of the out-take.

I'm not saying that popular taste is bad so that what's left over from the bad taste is good: I'm saying that what's left over is probably bad, but if you can take it and make it good or at least interesting, then you're not wasting as much as you would otherwise. You're recycling work and you're recycling people, and you're running your business as a by-product of other businesses. Of other *directly competitive* businesses, as a matter of fact. So that's a very economical operating procedure. It's also the funniest operating procedure because, as I said, leftovers are inherently funny.

Living in New York City gives people real incentives to want things that nobody else wants – to want all the leftover things. There are so many people here to compete with that changing your tastes to what other people don't want is your only hope of getting anything. For instance, on beautiful, sunny days in New York, it gets so crowded outside you can't even see Central Park through all the bodies. But very early on Sunday mornings in horrible rainy weather, when no one wants to get up and no one wants to get out even if they *are* up, you can go out and walk all over and have the streets to yourself and it's wonderful.

When we didn't have the money to do feature movies with thousands of cuts and retakes, etc., I tried to simplify the movie-making procedure, so I made movies where we used every foot of film that we shot, because it was cheaper, and easier and funnier. Also so we wouldn't have any leftovers ourselves. Then in 1969 we started editing our movies, but even with our own movies, I still love the leftovers best. The out-takes are all great. I'm scrupulously saving them.

I deviate from my philosophy of using leftovers in two areas: (1) my pet, and (2) my food.

I know I should have gone to the pound for a pet, but instead I bought one. It just happened. I saw him and I fell in love with him and I bought him, so there my emotions made me abandon my style.

I also have to admit that I can't tolerate eating leftovers. Food is my great extravagance. I really spoil myself, but then I try to compensate by scrupulously saving all of my food leftovers and bringing them into the office or leaving them in the street and recycling them there. My conscience won't let me throw anything out, even when I don't want it for myself. As I said, I really spoil myself in the food area, so my leftovers are often grand – my hairdresser's cat eats pâté at least twice a week. The leftovers usually turn out to be meat because I'll buy a huge piece of meat, cook it up for dinner, and then right before it's done I'll break down and have what I wanted for dinner in the first place – bread and jam. I'm only kidding myself when I go through the motions of cooking protein: all I ever really want is *sugar*. The rest is strictly for appearances, i.e., you can't take a princess to dinner and order a cookie for starters, no matter how much you crave one. People expect you to eat protein and you do so they won't talk. (If you decided to be stubborn and ordered the cookie, you'd wind up having to talk about why you want it and your philosophy of eating a cookie for dinner. And that would be too much trouble, so you order lamb and forget about what you really want.)

I did my first tape recording in 1964. I'm trying right now to remember the exact circumstances of what I made my first tape recording of. I remember who it was of, but I can't remember why I was carrying a tape recorder around with me that day or even why I had gone out and bought one. I think it all started because I was trying to do a book. A friend had written me a note saying that everybody we knew was writing a book, so that made me want to keep up and do one too. So I bought that tape recorder and I taped the most interesting person I knew at the time, Ondine, for a whole day. I was curious about all these new people I was meeting who could stay up for weeks at a time without ever going to sleep. I thought, 'These people are so imaginative. I just want to know what they do, why they're so imaginative and creative, talking all the time, always busy, full of energy . . . how come they can stay up so late and not be tired,' and pretty soon it would be four days later. I was determined to stay up all day and all night and tape Ondine, the most talkative and energetic of them all. But somewhere along the line I got tired, so I had to finish taping the rest of the twenty-four hours on a couple of other days. So actually, A, my novel, was a fraud, since it was billed as a consecutive twenty-four-hour tape-recorded 'novel', but it was actually taped on a few separate occasions. I used twenty tapes for it because I was using the small cassettes. And right at that point some kids came by the studio and asked if they could do some work, so I asked them to transcribe and type my novel, and it took them a year and a half to type up one day! That seems incredible to me now because I know that if they'd been any good they could have finished it in a week. I would glance over at them sometimes with admiration because they had me convinced that typing was one of the slowest, most painstaking jobs in the world. Now I realize that what I had were leftover typists, but I didn't know it then. Maybe they just liked being around all the people who hung around at the studio.

Another thing I couldn't understand was all those people who never slept who were always announcing, 'Oh I'm hitting my ninth day and it's glorious!' So I thought, 'Maybe it's time to do a movie about somebody who sleeps all night.' But I only had a camera that had three minutes on it, so I had to change the camera every three minutes to shoot three minutes. I slowed down the movie to make up for all the three minutes I lost changing the film, and we ran it at a slower speed to make up for the film I didn't shoot.

I suppose I have a really loose interpretation of 'work', because I think that just being alive is so much work at something you don't always want to do. Being born is like being kidnapped. And then sold into slavery. People are working every minute. The machinery is always going. Even when you sleep.

The hardest work I ever had to do mentally was go to court and get insulted by a lawyer. You're really on your own when you're up there on the witness stand and your friends can't stand up for you and everything's quiet except for you and the lawyer, and the lawyer's insulting you and you have to let him.

I loved working when I worked at commercial art and they told you what to do and how to do it and all you had to do was correct it and they'd say yes or no. The hard thing is when you have to dream up the tasteless things to do on your own. When I think about what sort of person I would most like to have on a retainer, I think it would be a boss. A boss who could tell me what to do, because that makes everything easy when you're working.

Unless you have a job where you have to do what somebody else tells you to do, then the only 'person' qualified to be your boss would be a computer that was programmed especially for you, that would take into consideration all of your finances, prejudices, quirks, idea potential, temper tantrums, talents, personality conflicts, growth rate desired, amount and nature of competition, what you'll eat for breakfast on the day you have to fulfill a contract, who you're jealous of, etc. A lot of people could help me with parts and segments of the business, but only a computer would be totally useful to me.

If I had a good computer I could catch up with my thoughts over the weekend if I ever got behind myself. A computer would be a very qualified boss.

Something I'm not doing these days that I should be doing is meeting more science people. I think that the best dinner party would be where each guest was required to bring a new piece of science news to the dinner table with him. Afterwards, you wouldn't feel you'd wasted any time feeding your machinery with just pieces of food. Nothing about diseases, though. Just pure science news.

People send me so many presents in the mail, but I wish that instead of all the presents and art mailers I would get science mailers in language I could understand. That would make me want to open my mail again.

When I'm working on a business project, I expect bad things to happen all the time. I always expect deals to fall through in the biggest, worst way possible. I guess I shouldn't worry, though. If something's going to happen for you, it will, you can't make it happen. And it never does happen until you're past the point where you care whether it happens or not. An actress friend told me that after she didn't want money any more and after she didn't want jewels any more, that's when she got money and jewels. I guess it's for our own good that it always happens that way, because after you stop wanting things is when having them won't make you go crazy. After you stop wanting them is when you can handle having them. Or before. But never during. If you get things when you really want them, you go crazy. Everything becomes distorted when something you really want is sitting in your lap.

After being alive, the next hardest work is having sex. Of course, for some people it isn't work because they need the exercise and they've got the energy for the sex and the sex gives them even more energy. Some people *get* energy from sex and some people *lose* energy from sex. I have found that it's too much work. But if you have the time for it, and if you need that exercise – then you should do it. But you could really save yourself a lot of trouble either way by first figuring out whether you're an energy-getter or an energy-loser. As I said, I'm an energy-loser. But I can understand it when I see people running around trying to get some.

It's just as much work for an attractive person *not to have* sex as for an *un*attractive person *to have* sex, so it's helpful if the attractive people happen to get energy from sex and if the unattractive people happen to lose energy from sex, because then their wants will fit in with the direction that people are pushing them in.

Along with having sex, being sexed is also hard work. I wonder whether it's harder for (1) a man to be a man, (2) a man to be a woman, (3) a woman to be a woman, or (4) a woman to be a man.

I don't really know the answer, but from watching all the different types, I know that the people who think they're working the hardest are the men who are trying to be women. They do double-time. They do all the double things: they think about shaving and not shaving, of primping and not primping, of buying men's clothes and women's clothes. I guess it's interesting to try to be another sex, but it can be exciting to just be your own sex.

A friend really hit it when he said, 'Frigid people really make it.' Frigid people don't have the standard emotional problems that hold so many people back and keep them from making it. When I was in my early twenties and had just gotten out of school, I could see that I wasn't frigid enough to not let problems keep me from working.

I thought that young people had more problems than old people, and I hoped I could last until I was older so I wouldn't have all those problems. Then I looked around and saw that everybody who looked young had young problems and that everybody who looked old had old problems. The 'old' problems to me looked easier to take than the 'young' problems. So I decided to go gray so nobody would know how old I was and I would look younger to them than how old they *thought* I was. I would gain a lot by going gray: (1) I would have old problems, which were easier to take than young problems, (2) everyone would be impressed by how young I looked, and (3) I would be relieved of the responsibility of acting young – I could occasionally lapse into eccentricity or senility and no one would think anything of it because of my gray hair. When you've got gray hair, every move you make seems 'young' and 'spry', instead of just being normally active. It's like you're getting a new talent. So I dyed my hair gray when I was about twenty-three or twenty-four.

Something that I look for in an associate is a certain amount of misunderstanding of what I'm trying to do. Not a fundamental misunderstanding; just minor misunderstandings here and there. When someone doesn't quite completely understand what you

94

want from them, or when they didn't quite hear what you told them to do, or when the tape is bad, or when their own fantasies start coming through, I often wind up liking what comes out of it all better than I liked my original idea. Then if you take what the first person who misunderstood you did, and you give that to someone else and tell them to make it more like how they know you would want it, that's good, too. If people never misunderstand you, and if they do everything exactly the way you tell them to, they're just transmitters of your ideas, and you get bored with that. But when you work with people who misunderstand you, instead of getting *transmissions* you get *transmutations*, and that's much more interesting in the long run.

I like the people who work for me to have their own ideas about things so they don't bore me, but then I like them to be enough like me to keep me company. I like to be tucked in, but I don't like to be tucked away.

They should have a college course now for maids and call it something glamorous, I think. People don't want to work at something unless there's a glamorous name tagged to it. The idea of America is theoretically so great because we've gotten rid of maids and janitors, but then, somebody still has to do it. I always think that even very intelligent people could get a lot out of being maids because they'd see so many interesting people and be working in the most beautiful houses. I mean, everybody does something for everybody else – your shoemaker does your shoes for you, and you do entertainment for him – it's always an exchange, and if it weren't for the stigma we give certain jobs, the exchange would always be equal. A mother is always doing things for her child, so what's wrong with a person off the street doing things for you? But there'll always be people who don't clean who think they're better than the people who do clean.

I've always thought that the President could do so much here to help change images. If the President would go into a public bathroom in the Capitol, and have the TV cameras film him cleaning the toilets and saying 'Why not? Somebody's got to do it!' then that would do so much for the morale of the people who do the wonderful job of keeping the toilets clean. I mean, it is a wonderful thing that they're doing.

The President has so much good publicity potential that hasn't been exploited. He should just sit down one day and make a list of all the things that people are embarrassed to do that they shouldn't be embarrassed to do, and then do them all on television.

Sometimes B and I fantasize about what I would do if I were President – how I would use my TV time.

Airline stewardesses have the best public image – hostesses in the air. Their work is actually what the waitresses in Bickford's do, plus a few additional duties. I don't want to put down the airline stewardesses, I just want to put up the Bickford ladies. The difference is that airline stewardessing is a New World job that never had to contend with any class stigmas left over from the Old World peasant–aristocracy syndrome.

What's great about this country is that America started the tradition where the richest consumers buy essentially the same things as the poorest. You can be watching TV and see Coca-Cola, and you can know that the President drinks Coke, Liz Taylor drinks Coke, and just think, you can drink Coke, too. A Coke is a Coke and no amount of money can get you a better Coke than the one the bum on the corner is drinking. All the Cokes are the same and all the Cokes are good. Liz Taylor knows it, the President knows it, the bum knows it, and you know it.

In Europe the royalty and the aristocracy used to eat a lot better than the peasants – they weren't eating the same things at all. It was either partridge or porridge, and each class stuck to its own food. But when Queen Elizabeth came here and President Eisenhower bought her a hot dog I'm sure he felt confident that she couldn't have had delivered to Buckingham Palace a better hot dog than that one he bought her for maybe twenty cents at the ballpark. Because there *is* no better hot dog than a ballpark hot dog. Not for a dollar, not for ten dollars, not for a hundred thousand dollars could she get a better hot dog. She could get one for twenty cents and so could anybody else.

Sometimes you fantasize that people who are really up-there and rich and living it up have something you don't have, that their things must be better than your things because they have more money than you. But they drink the same Cokes and eat the same hot dogs and wear the same ILGWU clothes and see the same TV shows and the same movies. Rich people can't see a sillier version of *Truth or Consequences*, or a scarier version of *The Exorcist*. You can get just as revolted as they can – you can have the same nightmares. All of this is really American.

The idea of America is so wonderful because the more equal something is, the more American it is. For instance, a lot of places give you special treatment when you're famous, but that's not really American. The other day something *very* American happened to me. I was going into an auction at Parke-Bernet and they wouldn't let me in because I had my dog with me, so I had to wait in the lobby for the friend I was meeting there to tell him I'd been turned away. And while I was waiting in the lobby I signed autographs. It was a really American situation to be in.

(Also, by the way, the 'special treatment' sometimes works in reverse when you're famous. Sometimes people are mean to me because I'm Andy Warhol.)

Wherever it's possible, you should try to pay people in measurements that are the most suitable for their talent or job. A writer may want to get paid by the word, by the page, by the number of times the reader breaks down crying or bursts out laughing, by the chapter, by the number of new ideas introduced, by the book, or by the year, just to name a few possible categories. A director may want to get paid by the movie or by the foot or by the number of times a Chevrolet appears in the frames.

I'm still thinking about maids. It really has to do with how you're raised. Some people just aren't embarrassed by the idea of somebody else cleaning up after them, and, even though I talk

97

about being a maid not being any different from any other job – because I know it *shouldn't* be considered any different from any other job – still, somehow, deep down, I'm truly embarrassed at the idea of somebody cleaning up after me. If I were really able to think about being a maid the same way I think about, say, being a dentist, I wouldn't be any more embarrassed to let a maid clean up after me than I would be to let a dentist fix my teeth. (Actually, 'dentist' is a bad example, because I *am* embarrassed to let a dentist fix my teeth, especially if my skin is broken out and I'm sitting under those green lights. But I'll stick with that example because the embarrassment I feel about letting someone clean my teeth is nowhere near the embarrassment I feel when someone is around cleaning up after me.)

I confront the problem of how to look at a maid only when I'm staying at a European hotel or when I'm a guest at somebody else's house. It's so awkward when you come face to face with a maid. I've never been able to pull it off. Some people I know are very comfortable looking at maids and even telling them what they'd like done, but I can't handle it. When I go to a hotel, I find myself trying to stay there all day so the maid can't come in. I make a point of it. Because I just don't know where to put my eyes, where to look, what to be doing while they're cleaning. It's actually a lot of work, avoiding the maid, when I think about it.

When I was a child I never had a fantasy about having a maid, what I had a fantasy about having was candy. As I matured that fantasy translated itself into 'make money to have candy', because as you get older, of course, you get more realistic. Then, after my third nervous breakdown and I still didn't have that extra candy, my career started to pick up, and I started getting more and more candy, and now I have a roomful of candy all in shopping bags. So, as I'm thinking about it now, my success got me a candy room instead of a maid's room. As I said, it all depends on what your fantasies as a kid were, whether you're able to look at a maid or not. Because of what my fantasies were, I'm now a lot more comfortable looking at a Hershey Bar.

It's strange the way having money isn't much. You take three people to a restaurant and you pay three hundred dollars. Okay. Then you take those same three people to a corner shop – shoppe – and get everything there. You got just as filled at the corner shoppe as at the grand restaurant – more, actually – and it cost you only fifteen or twenty dollars, and you had basically the same food.

I was trying to think the other day about what you do now in America if you want to be successful. Before, you were dependable and wore a good suit. Looking around, I guess that today you have to do all the same things but not wear a good suit. I guess that's all it is. Think rich. Look poor.

7 Time

A   I always think about the people who build buildings and then they're not around any more. Or a movie with a crowd scene and everybody's dead. It's frightening.

I try to think of what time is and all I can think is . . .
'Time is time was.'

People say 'time on my hands', Well, I looked at my hands and I
saw a lot of lines. And then somebody told me that some people
don't have lines. I didn't believe her. We were sitting in a
restaurant and she said, 'How can you say that? Look at that
waiter over there!' She called him over, 'Honey! Honey? Can
you bring me a glass of water?' and when he brought it she
grabbed his hand and showed it to me and it had no lines! Just
the three main ones. And she said, 'See? I told you. Some people
like that waiter have no lines.' And I thought, 'Gee, I wish I was
a waiter.'

    If the lines on your hand are wrinkles, it must mean your hands
worry a lot.

Sometimes you're invited to a big ball and for months you think
about how glamorous and exciting it's going to be. Then you fly
to Europe and you go to the ball and when you think back on it
a couple of months later what you remember is maybe the car
ride to the ball, you can't remember the ball at all. Sometimes
the little times you don't think are anything while they're
happening turn out to be what marks a whole period of your life.
I should have been dreaming for months about the car ride to
the ball and getting dressed for the car ride, and buying my
ticket to Europe so I could take the car ride. Then, who knows,
maybe I could have remembered the ball.

Some people decide to be old and then they do exactly what old
people are supposed to do. But when they were twenty years old
they were doing what twenty-year-olds are supposed to do. And
then there are those other people who look twenty all their
lives. It's thrilling to see movie stars – since they're more involved

in that than most people – who have worked on their beauty, who still have all their energy because they're still working with their young selves.

Since people are going to be living longer and getting older, they'll just have to learn how to be babies longer. I think that's what's happening now. Some kids I know personally are staying babies longer.

I was standing on a street in Paris once and this old lady was looking at me, and I thought, 'Oh she's probably staring at me because she's English,' because English people always know me from a London television disaster that somehow starred me. So I sort of looked away and she said, 'Aren't you Andy?' I said yes and she said, 'You came to my house in Provincetown twenty-eight and a half years ago. You were wearing a sunhat. You don't even remember me, but I'll never forget you in that sunhat. You see, you couldn't take any sun.' I felt so strange because I couldn't remember at all and she remembered to the month. Because to remember 'twenty-eight and a half years ago' without even stopping to calculate must mean that she really kept track and would say, 'Well it's nineteen years now since he was here in the sunhat.' It was very peculiar – her husband was there and they were disagreeing about how long it was. He said, 'No no no. We weren't married yet, remember? So it must have been twenty-six and three-quarter years ago.'

Some people say Paris is more esthetic than New York. Well, in New York you don't have time to have an esthetic because it takes half the day to go downtown and half the day to go uptown.

Then there's time in the street, when you run into somebody you haven't seen in, say, five years and you play it all on one level. When you see each other and you don't even lose a beat, that's when it's the best. You don't say 'What have you been doing?' – you don't try to catch up. Maybe you mention that you're on your way to 8th Street to get a frozen custard and

104

maybe they mention which movie they're on their way to see, but that's it. Just a casual check-in. Very light, cool, off-hand, very American. Nobody's fazed, nobody's thrown out of time, nobody gets hysterical, nobody loses a beat. That's when it's good. And then when somebody asks you whatever happened to so-and-so you just say, 'Yes, I saw him having a malted on 53rd Street.' Just play it all on one level, like everything was yesterday.

I think I'm missing some chemicals and that's why I have this tendency to be more of a – mama's boy. A – sissy. No, a mama's boy. A 'butterboy', I think I'm missing some responsibility chemicals and some reproductive chemicals. If I had them I would probably think more about aging the right way and being married four times and having a family – wives and children and dogs. I'm immature, but maybe something could happen to my chemicals and I could get mature. I could start getting wrinkles and stop wearing my wings.

They always say that time changes things, but you actually have to change them yourself.

Sometimes people let the same problem make them miserable for years when they could just say, 'So what.' That's one of my favorite things to say. 'So what.'
    'My mother didn't love me.' So what.
    'My husband won't ball me.' So what.
    'I'm a success but I'm still alone.' So what.
    I don't know how I made it through all the years before I learned how to do that trick. It took a long time for me to learn it, but once you do, you never forget.

What makes a person spend time being sad when they could be happy? I was in the Far East and I was walking down a path and there was a big happy party going on, and actually they were burning a person to death. They were having a party and they were happy, singing and dancing.
    Then the other day I was on the Bowery and a person in a

flophouse jumped out of the window and died, and a crowd went around the body, and then a bum staggered over and said, 'Did you see the comedy across the street?'

I'm not saying you should be happy when a person dies, but just that it's curious to see cases that prove you don't *have* to be sad about it, depending on what you think it means, and what you think about what you think it means.

A person can cry or laugh. Always when you're crying you could be laughing, you have the choice. Crazy people know how to do this best because their minds are loose. So you can take the flexibility your mind is capable of and make it work for you. You decide what you want to do and how you want to spend your time. Remember, though, that I think I'm missing some chemicals, so it's easier for me than for a person who has a lot of responsibility chemicals, but the same principle could still be applied in a lot of instances.

At the end of my time, when I die, I don't want to leave any leftovers. And I don't want to be a leftover. I was watching TV this week and I saw a lady go into a ray machine and disappear. That was wonderful, because matter is energy and she just dispersed. That could be a really American invention, the best American invention – to be able to disappear. I mean, that way they couldn't say you died, they couldn't say you were murdered, they couldn't say you committed suicide over somebody.

The worst thing that could happen to you after the end of your time would be to be embalmed and laid up in a pyramid. I'm repulsed when I think about the Egyptians taking each organ and embalming it separately in its own receptacle. I want my machinery to disappear.

Still, I do really like the idea of people turning into sand or something, so the machinery keeps working after you die. I guess disappearing would be shirking work that your machinery still had left to do. Since I believe in work, I guess I shouldn't think about disappearing when I die. And anyway, it would be very glamorous to be reincarnated as a big ring on Pauline de Rothschild's finger.

I really do live for the future, because when I'm eating a box of candy, I can't wait to taste the last piece. I don't even taste any of the other pieces, I just want to finish and throw the box away and not have to have it on my mind any more.

I would rather either have it now or know I'll never have it so I don't have to think about it.

That's why some days I wish I were very very old-looking so I wouldn't have to think about getting old-looking.

I really look awful, and I never bother to primp up or try to be appealing because I just don't want anyone to get involved with me. And that's the truth. I play down my good features and play up the bad ones. So I look awful and I wear the wrong pants and the wrong shoes and I come at the wrong time with the wrong friends, and I say the wrong things and I talk to the wrong person, and then *still* sometimes somebody gets interested and I freak out and I wonder, 'What did I do wrong?' So then I go home and try to figure it out. 'Well I must be wearing something that somebody thinks is attractive. I'd better change it. Before things get too far.' So I go over to my three-way mirror and I study myself and I see that I have fifteen new pimples on my face and ordinarily that should have stopped them. So I think, 'How weird. I know I look bad. I made myself look especially bad – especially wrong – because I knew a lot of the right people would be there, and still someone somehow got interested . . .' Then I start to panic because I think I don't know what's attractive that I should eliminate before it starts causing me any more trouble. You see, to get to know one more person is just too hard, because each new person takes up more time and space. The way to keep some of your time to yourself is to maintain yourself so unattractively that nobody else is interested in any of it.

I look at professional people like comedians in night-clubs, and I'm always impressed with their perfect timing, but I could never understand how they can bear to say exactly the same thing all the time. Then I realized what's the difference, because you're always repeating your same things all the time anyway, whether or not somebody asks you or it's your job. You're usually making the same mistakes. You apply your usual mistakes to every new category or field you go into.

Whenever I'm interested in something, I know the timing's off, because I'm always interested in the right thing at the wrong time. I should just be getting interested after I'm not interested any more, because right after I'm embarrassed to still be thinking about a certain idea, that's when the idea is just about to make somebody a few million dollars. My same good mistakes.

I learned something about time when I used to have to go around New York and see people by appointment in their offices. Somebody would give me an appointment at ten o'clock, so I'd beat my brains out to get there at exactly ten, and I would get there and they wouldn't see me until five minutes to one. So when you go through this a hundred times and you hear, 'Ten o'clock?' you say, 'Weeeelll, that sounds funny, I think I'll show up at five minutes to one.' So I used to show up at five minutes to one and it always worked. That's when I would see the person. So I learned. It was like being a laboratory rat and they put you through all those tests and you get rewarded when you do it right, and when you do it wrong you're kicked back, so you learn. So I learned when people would be around.

The only time my system didn't work was with Liz Taylor. I was in Rome appearing in a movie with her and for a week every day she was hours late for shooting, and finally I thought, 'Well listen, let's just take our time tomorrow and not get up at six-thirty.' So that day she got there before everybody else. She was there before the wardrobe lady and the key grip. She practically had the coffee perking. She really keeps you on your toes. She did the same thing I did, in reverse, and I was thrown off because I didn't know her well enough to predict her. Liz Taylor, in being late fifty times and then early once, must be applying the same principle that I do by having my hair gray so when I do something with a normal amount of energy it seems 'young'. Liz Taylor when she's on time seems 'early'. It's like you get a new talent all of a sudden by being so bad at something for so long, and then suddenly one day being not quite so bad.

I like the idea that people in New York now have to wait in line for movies. You go by so many theaters where there are long, long lines. But nobody looks unhappy about it. It costs so much money just to live now, and if you're on a date, you can spend your whole date time in line, and that way it saves you money because you don't have to think of other things to do while you're waiting and you get to know your person, and you suffer a little together, and then you're entertained for two hours. So you've gotten very close, you've shared a complete experience. And the idea of waiting for something makes it more exciting anyway. Never getting in is the most exciting, but after that waiting to get in is the most exciting.

If I only had time for one vacation every ten years I still don't think I'd want to go anywhere. I'd probably just go to my room, fluff up the pillow, turn on a couple of TVs, open a box of Ritz crackers, break the seal on a box of Russell Stovers, sit down with the latest issue of every magazine except *TV Guide* from the corner news-stand, then pick up the phone and call everybody I know to ask them to look in their *TV Guides* to tell me what's on, what's been on, what's going to be on. I also enjoy rereading the newspaper. Especially in Paris. I can't reread the international *Herald Tribune* enough when I'm in Paris. I love to while away the hours while other people do their meanwhiles, as long as they call in to report. In my room, time moves so slowly for me, it's only outside that everything is happening so fast.

I don't like to travel, because I really like slow time and for a plane you have to leave three or four hours ahead of time, so that's a day right there. If you really want your life to pass like a movie in front of you, just travel, you can forget your life.

I like a rut. People call me up and say, 'I hope I'm not disturbing your rut, calling you up like this.' They know how much I like it.

One mistake I make time after time is not following the Golden Rule: I hold elevators. Also, even though I try to throw things away and simplify my life, I palm things off on other people.

What makes a movie fast is when you see it, and then when you see it a second time it goes really fast. If you really want to suffer, go see something and then go see it again. You'll see that your suffering goes by quicker the second time.

I can see a murder mystery one night, and then see it a second time the next night and still not know who did it until the very last minute. So I know there's something *really wrong* with me. I mean, if I can sit there and watch another *Thin Man* and watch it again the next night, and still not know who the murderer is again until the very last minute . . . And I'll be just as curious and just as on-the-edge-of-my-chair waiting to find out, and just as shocked as I was the night before. If I've seen it fifteen times, then *maybe* one time out of the fifteen it'll come back to me and I might get a glimmer of who did it. I guess time is actually the best plot – the suspense of seeing if you'll remember.

Digital clocks and watches really show me that there's a new time on my hand. And it's sort of frightening. Somebody has thought of a new way to show time, so I guess we won't be saying one 'o'clock' too much longer, because that's 'of the clock' or 'by the clock' and there won't be any more clocks: it'll be 'one time' instead of 'one o'clock' and 'three-thirty time' and 'four-forty-five time'.

When I was little and I was sick a lot, those sick times were like little intermissions. Innermissions. Playing with dolls.

I never used to cut out my cut-out dolls. Some people who've worked with me might suggest that I had someone else cut them out for me, but really the reason I didn't cut them out was that I didn't want to ruin the nice pages they were on. I always left my cut-out dolls in my cut-out books.

About Time
　From time to time
　　Do time
　　　Time yourself

　　weekends.

　　　In time
　　　　In no time
　　　　　In good time
　　　　　　Between time
　　　　　　　Time and again
　　　　　　　Lifetime
　　　　　　　Time-worn

　　　　　　Pass time
　　　　　　Mark time
　　　　　　Buy time
　　　　　　Keep time

　　　　　　　On time
　　　　　　　In time
　　　　　　　　Time off
　　　　　　　　Time out
　　　　　　　　Time in
　　　　　　　　Time card
　　　　　　　　Time lapse
　　　　　　　　Time zone

　　　　　The beforetime
　　　　　The meantime
　　　　　The aftertime
　　　　　The All-time—

When I look around today, the biggest anachronism I see is pregnancy. I just can't believe that people are still pregnant.

The best time for me is when I don't have any problems that I can't buy my way out of.

8 Death

A I'm so sorry to hear about it. I just thought that things were magic and that it would never happen.

I don't believe in it, because you're not around to know that it's happened. I can't say anything about it because I'm not prepared for it.

9 Economics

A   If you're a Rockefeller, New York is really your town.
Can you imagine?

don't understand anything except GREEN BILLS. Not negotiable bonds, not personal checks, not Traveller's Checks.

And if you give anybody a hundred-dollar bill in the SUPERMARKET, they *call the manager.*

Money is SUSPICIOUS, because people think you're not supposed to have it, even if you do have it.

I'm PARANOID now when I go to D'Agostino's because I always have another SHOPPING BAG with me and they tell you that you have to check it, but I won't. A lady doesn't have to check her pocketbook, so I won't check my bag. It's principle. So then I'm paranoid they'll think I'm stealing, so I hold my head up high and LOOK RICH. Because I don't steal. I go right to the dairy counter with all my money and I'm so happy because I'm going to go down all the counters and buy things for my windowsill in my bedroom.

Rich people don't carry their money in wallets or Gucci this-es or Valentino thats. They carry their money in a business envelope. In a long business envelope. And the tens have a paper clip on them, so do the fives and twenties. And the money is usually new. It's sent over by special messenger from the bank offices – or their husbands' offices. They just sign for it. And it stays there until they have to dish out a twenty to their daughter.

The best way I like to carry money, actually, is messily. Crumpled wads. A paper bag is good.

One day I was having lunch with a princess and she had this little SCOTCH PURSE that was in the motif of a PLAID CAP with a POM-POM. We were at the Women's Exchange on Madison Avenue. And she took this crisp money out of her purse and she said, 'You see? I fold it in the Rothschild manner. It lasts longer that way. I've been doing it all my life.' She folded each bill separately, lengthwise, and then folded it again lengthwise. All new money. All in a little stack. The theory is that it lasts longer. That's the Rothschild way of folding money – that you can't see it.

That's *The Rothschild Story*.

I had a very good French wallet that I bought in Germany for a hundred and fifty dollars. For the big money. The big-size foreign money. But then in New York it ripped and I took it to the shoemaker and by mistake he stitched up the part where you put the paper money, so I can only use it now for change.

Cash. I just am not happy when I don't have it. The minute I have it I have to spend it. And I just buy STUPID THINGS.

Checks aren't money.

When I have fifty or sixty dollars in my pocket, I can go into Brentano's and buy *The Life Of Rose Kennedy* and say, 'May I please have a register receipt?'

And the more receipts I get, the bigger the thrill. They're even getting to be like money to me now.

And when I go to the numbers-racket newspaper greeting card store in the neighborhood because it's late and everything else is closed, I go in and I'm very CHIC. Because I have money. I buy *Harper's Bazaar* and then I ask for a receipt. The newsboy yells at me and then he writes it on plain white paper. I won't accept that. 'List the magazines, please. And put the date. And write the name of the store at the top.' That makes it feel even more like money. The reason for doing it is I want that man to know I am an HONEST CITIZEN, and I SAVE MY STUBS and I PAY MY TAXES.

Then I go and eat, just because I have money, not because I'm hungry. I have it and I have to spend it before I go to sleep. So if it's one in the morning and I'm still awake, I take a cab to the all-night pharmacy and buy whatever I've been brainwashed with that night on TV.

I'll buy anything in a drugstore in the middle of the night. I'll make the store stay open a little late for me while I finish up, because they know I have money, so that's prestige. Right? The next step is getting to know the store so well they let me charge. I tell the store I don't like to get bills in the mail because it DEPRESSES ME. 'Just tell me what I owe you now,' I say, 'and I'll come back next week when I have more cash and pay you. Give me a bill, and when I bring it back you can mark it PAID.'

After you PAY SOMEBODY BACK you never run into them any more. But before that, they're EVERYWHERE.

When I have a lot of money, my tips are just ridiculous. If the fare comes to a dollar thirty, you know, I say just keep two dollars ... But if I don't have money, I ask for twenty cents back.

I gave a cab driver a hundred dollars once. In the dark I thought it was a dollar. The fare was sixty cents (this is before the fares went up the last time) and I told him to keep it. And that's always depressed me.

I sometimes get into a cab without money and go someplace to pick up some money. To the bank or to the office or to pick up some that's been left for me with a doorman. Now, on the way up in the cab without any money, I would have to do such an act with the cab driver. He's got that plastic divider-shield up which automatically makes you feel like a criminal – that you're going to shoot him or hold him up. So you've got to really convince that guy and make him like you, that you're just picking up an envelope with the doorman. So I say, 'I'll leave my paper bag with you.' But then I write down their license number in case they split and I run in to get my envelope. On a certain run that I make a lot, I usually pick up the envelope and then go next door to the stationery store to cash it. If they can't cash it, I have to go next door to Riker's. They can never cash it. Then the tie shop. They can always cash it. Then I get back in and I say to the driver, 'Take me back where I came from.' Well, that little trip has cost me half of what I've gone to pick up (with the tip that I'd already promised the driver). So then I have to go and blow money in a health food store. I blow some on pink organic toothpaste, because it brought back memories of Elizabeth

121

Arden's pink toothpaste. I want to find something that tastes like the old-fashioned Ipana in the yellow tube.

I only take cabs because I like to talk. If they don't put the meter on, halfway through the ride I ask them, 'Why don't you turn the meter on?' 'Well, it's such a short trip, I thought—' I say, 'You thought, you thought! If you had said to me, "Can I make it on my own?" I would have said sure, given you what it would have cost and a tip besides. Now we're here, and there's nothing on the meter, and by rights I don't owe you anything.' And at that they have to say, 'No . . .' So I drop a quarter in. I say, 'You see? It's better to ask. You can't beat the system.'

You can't talk on the news yet about how to beat the system, and that's what people want to know about.

It's great to buy friends. I don't think there's anything wrong with having a lot of money and attracting people with it. Look who you're attracting: EVERYBODY!

I know somebody who is very rich and all day long his paranoia is that people are only around him for his money. But then, he's always the first to tell you he's just flown in his private plane to Washington, D.C., but took a commercial airline to L.A.

If you look like a rag, but if you've got fifteen dollars in your pocket, you can still impress people that you've got money. All you have to do is go down to the liquor store and buy a bottle of champagne. You can impress a whole roomful of people and with luck maybe you'll never see them again, so they'll always think you've got money. I never can have money and pretend I'm poor. I can only be poor and pretend I'm rich.

I know a woman who calls somebody up every afternoon and says, 'I'll pay you a hundred dollars to fuck me.' Fabulous. She makes sure they're very attractive and from good families and everything, but they need maybe a few more dollars to spend on wheels for their Mercedes. This girl does not have diamonds, nothing she wears costs that much, and yet there's 'money' in her nose and in her ears and in her brain. It's in her cheekbones, too, it gives her structure. A delivery man from the coffee shop might come in and you could ask him, 'Look at her. Is she poor or rich?' And he'd know. Because the face is 'money'. She can be walking down the street smoking a cigarette and she can hail a cab in just such a dainty way that the whole affair changes.

I hate Sundays: there's nothing open except plant stores and bookstores.

Money is money. It doesn't matter if I've worked hard or easy for it. I spend it the same.

I like money on the wall. Say you were going to buy a $200,000 painting. I think you should take that money, tie it up, and hang it on the wall. Then when someone visited you the first thing they would see is the money on the wall.

I don't think everybody should have money. It shouldn't be for everybody – you wouldn't know who was important. How boring. Who would you gossip about? Who would you put down? Never that great feeling of somebody saying 'Can I borrow twenty-five dollars?'

Christmas is when you have to go to the bank and get crisp money to put in envelopes from the stationery store for tips. After you tip the doorman, he goes on sick leave or quits and the new one isn't impressed.

I love to get the best orchestra seat for a Broadway show, leave after the first act, and catch the end of the show next door, the best seat there, too. And I have two stubs. That's work because I'm 'covering' it.

I was never interested in a plain checkbook – I only wanted the desk model because that has a lot of status, I think.

LYING IN THE BATHTUB WITH A PILLOW BEHIND MY HEAD MAKES ME FEEL VERY RICH – the pillow that I sent away for for $3.95 and a boxtop. Maybe it's an illusion. Of grandeur. But when you pay the phone bills every month that I do, you know you have the money.

123

It's fun to buy a lot of things for a little. To get a big shopping bag in Lamston's – to pay the thirty cents for the bag, and then to *fill* it. You've blown maybe sixty dollars in Lamston's, and you get home and you put everything on the bed and you take the Comet and you wash the prices on the tops off where it's written '$1.69'. Then, the minute you've put all the stuff away, you want to go shopping again. So you go to the Village. You turn your nose up at one plant shop because you want them to think you're going to the expensive plant shop across the street. And then you want to impress that plant man, so you go in and you say, 'I'll take it.' Then you bring those home and your room is filled with flowers. That makes you feel so rich you want to leave your door open just a crack so the people across the hall can see you're rich. Not enough so you think they're going to rob you, though.

When I had a lot of cash once, I sprang for my first color television. The 'tingle' in black and white was driving me crazy. I thought maybe if I saw all the commercials in color they'd look new and I'd have more things to go out and buy again.

Korvettes. In cash. I even wanted remote control, but that was in another department. I started taking it home, but then I got paranoid. The box said 'Sony' and 'Korvettes' and I wanted it to say 'Lamston's', because I was taking it up my elevator, up my hall, into my apartment, and with that wrapping, and with having to throw out the white styrofoam that shows its shape,I thought, 'I won't have this for long.'

Can't I deduct liquor if I have to get high to talk and talking's my business?

I have a Fantasy about Money: I'm walking down the street and I hear somebody say – in a whisper – 'There goes the richest person in the world.'

I don't look at dates on nickels. It could be from 1910, I wouldn't save it. I'd spend it with a dime for a Clark Bar.

I hate PENNIES. I wish they'd stop making them altogether. I would never save them. I don't have the time. I like to say in stores, 'Oh forget it, keep those pennies. It makes my French wallet too heavy.'

CHANGE can get to be a burden, but it can also come in very handy when you have no money. You hunt for it, you look under the BED, you go through all the COAT POCKETS, saying, 'Maybe I left a quarter *there* or *there* . . .' Sometimes it can be the difference between buying a PACK OF CIGARETTES or not, to only be able to dig up sixty-nine cents instead of seventy cents. You HUNT and HUNT and HUNT for that LAST PENNY. The only time YOU LIKE A PENNY is when you need ONE MORE.

And then they ask you in the stores, 'Do you have a penny?' and then you have to go SCROUNGING. Or else you do have a penny but you just don't feel like looking . . .

I asked a cabbie the other day what money meant to him. 'Good times,' he said. 'I take my wife out, I enjoy my wife, I enjoy going out with her, so when I have money I take her out.'

I feel the same way.

Then I asked this cabbie how he felt when people gave him pennies. 'Pennies? I never get pennies. – No, wait. I shouldn't say that. I got five pennies the other day from Gina Lollobrigida.'

I asked him to tell me about it.

'There's nothing to tell, she's a very nice person, she likes New York, she doesn't like Hollywood, she's traveling all over, I think she's left now, and she's writing a book.'

GINA LOLLOBRIGIDA.

If they made everything work out to be an even amount, pennies could be the weights on the bottom of the flowerpots.

Money is the MOMENT to me.

Money is my MOOD.

To some people money is to buy today what they think will have value tomorrow. GET IT CHEAP, they say. Well, I don't have anything that goes below 1955. I swear. Nothing. Maybe a pencil I borrow from somebody might be from 1947. You don't know.

125

American money is very well-designed, really. I like it better than any other kind of money. I've thrown it in the East River down by the Staten Island Ferry just to see it float.

What we're all looking for is someone who doesn't live there, just pays for it.

If I think something I buy is worth more money than I pay, and if I like the people I'm buying from, I have to tell them they're undercharging me. I don't feel right until I tell them. If I buy a sandwich that's very very filling, and if the person I buy it from doesn't know how great it is, I have to tell him.

I don't feel like I get germs when I hold money. Money has a certain kind of amnesty. I feel, when I'm holding money, that the dollar bill has no more germs on it than my hands do. When I pass my hand over money, it becomes perfectly clean to me. I don't know where it's been – who's touched it and with what – but that's all erased the moment I touch it.

10 Atmosphere

B I wanted to make a film that showed how sad and lyrical it is for those two old ladies to be living in those rooms full of newspapers and cats.

A You shouldn't make it sad. You should just say, 'This is how people today are doing things.'

Space is all one space and thought is all one thought, but my mind divides its spaces into spaces into spaces and thoughts into thoughts into thoughts. Like a large condominium. Occasionally I think about the one Space and the one Thought, but usually I don't. Usually I think about my condominium.

The condominium has hot and cold running water, a few Heinz pickles thrown in, some chocolate-covered cherries, and when the Woolworth's hot fudge sundae switch goes on, then I know I really have something.

(This condominium meditates a lot: it's usually closed for the afternoon, evening, and morning.)

Your mind makes spaces into spaces. It's a lot of hard work. A lot of hard spaces. As you get older you get more spaces, and more compartments. And more things to put in the compartments.

To be really rich, I believe, is to have one space. One big empty space.

I really believe in empty spaces, although, as an artist, I make a lot of junk.

Empty space is never-wasted space.

Wasted space is any space that has art in it.

An artist is somebody who produces things that people don't need to have but that he – for *some reason* – thinks it would be a good idea to give them.

Business Art is a much better thing to be making than Art Art, because Art Art doesn't support the space it takes up, whereas Business Art does. (If Business Art doesn't support its own space it goes out-of-business.)

So on the one hand I really believe in empty spaces, but on the other hand, because I'm still making some art, I'm still making junk for people to put in their spaces that I believe should be empty: i.e., I'm helping people *waste* their space when what I really want to do is help them *empty* their space.

I go even further in not following my own philosophy, because I can't even empty my own spaces. It's not that my philosophy is failing me, it's that I am failing my own philosophy. I breach what I preach more than I practice it.

When I look at things, I always see the space they occupy. I always want the space to reappear, to make a comeback, because it's lost space when there's something in it. If I see a chair in a beautiful space, no matter how beautiful the chair is, it can never be as beautiful to me as the plain space.

My favorite piece of sculpture is a solid wall with a hole in it to frame the space on the other side.

I believe that everyone should live in one big empty space. It can be a small space, as long as it's clean and empty. I like the Japanese way of rolling everything up and locking it away in cupboards. But I wouldn't even have the cupboards, because that's hypocritical. But if you can't go all the way and you really feel you need a closet, then your closet should be a totally separate piece of space so you don't use it as a crutch too much. If you live in New York, your closet should be, at the very least, in New Jersey. Aside from false dependency, another reason for keeping your closet at a good distance from where you live is that you don't want to feel you're living next door to your own dump. Another person's dump wouldn't bother you so much because you wouldn't know exactly what was in it, but thinking about your own closet, and knowing every little thing that's in it, could drive you crazy.

Everything in your closet should have an expiration date on it the way milk and bread and magazines and newspapers do, and once something passes its expiration date, you should throw it out.

What you should do is get a box for a month, and drop everything in it and at the end of the month lock it up. Then date
130

it and send it over to Jersey. You should try to keep track of it, but if you can't and you lose it, that's fine, because it's one less thing to think about, another load off your mind.

Tennessee Williams saves everything up in a trunk and then sends it out to a storage place. I started off myself with trunks and the odd pieces of furniture, but then I went around shopping for something better and now I just drop everything into the same-size brown cardboard boxes that have a color patch on the side for the month of the year. I really hate nostalgia, though, so deep down I hope they all get lost and I never have to look at them again. That's another conflict. I want to throw things right out the window as they're handed to me, but instead I say thank you and drop them into the box-of-the-month. But my other outlook is that I really do want to save things so they can be used again someday.

There should be supermarkets that sell things and supermarkets that buy things back, and until that equalizes, there'll be more waste than there should be. Everybody would always have something to sell back, so everybody would have money, because everybody would have something to sell. We all have something, but most of what we have isn't salable, there's such a preference today for brand new things. People should be able to sell their old cans, their old chicken bones, their old shampoo bottles, their old magazines. We have to get more organized. People who tell you we're running out of things are just making the prices go up higher. How can we be running out of anything when there's always, if I'm not mistaken, the same amount of matter in the Universe, with the exception of what goes into the black holes?

I think about people eating and going to the bathroom all the time, and I wonder why they don't have a tube up their behind that takes all the stuff they eat and recycles it back into their mouth, regenerating it, and then they'd never have to think about buying food or eating it. And they wouldn't even have to see it – it wouldn't even be dirty. If they wanted to, they could artificially color it on the way back in. Pink. (I got the idea from thinking that bees shit honey, but then I found out that honey isn't bee-shit, it's bee regurgitation, so the honeycombs aren't bee bathrooms as I had previously thought. The bees therefore must run off somewhere else to do it.)

Free countries are great, because you can actually sit in somebody else's space for a while and pretend you're a part of it. You can sit in the Plaza Hotel and you don't even have to live there. You can just sit and watch the people go by.

There are different ways for individual people to take over space – to command space. Very shy people don't even want to take up the space that their body actually takes up, whereas very outgoing people want to take up as much space as they can get.

Before media there used to be a physical limit on how much space one person could take up by themselves. People, I think, are the only things that know how to take up more space than the space they're actually in, because with media you can sit back and still let yourself fill up space on records, in the movies, most exclusively on the telephone and least exclusively on television.

Some people must go crazy when they realize how much space they've managed to command. If you were the star of the biggest show on television and took a walk down an average American street one night while you were on the air, and if you looked through windows and saw yourself on television in everybody's living room, taking up some of their space, can you imagine how you would feel?

I don't think anybody, no matter how famous they are in other fields, could ever feel as peculiar as a television star. Not even the biggest rock star whose records are playing on sound systems everywhere he goes could feel as peculiar as someone who knows he's on everybody's television regularly. No matter how small he is, he has all the space anyone could ever want, right there in the television box.

You should have contact with your closest friends through the most intimate and exclusive of all media – the telephone.

132

I've always had a conflict because I'm shy and yet I like to take up a lot of personal space. Mom always said, 'Don't be pushy, but let everybody know you're around.' I wanted to command more space than I was commanding, but then I knew I was too shy to know what to do with the attention if I did manage to get it. That's why I love television. That's why I feel that television is the media I'd most like to shine in. I'm really jealous of everybody who's got their own show on television.

As I said, I want a show of my own – called *Nothing Special*.

I'm impressed with people who can create new spaces with the right words. I only know one language, and sometimes in the middle of a sentence I feel like a foreigner trying to talk it because I have word spasms where the parts of some words begin to sound peculiar to me and in the middle of saying the word I'll think, 'Oh, this can't be right – this sounds very peculiar, I don't know if I should try to finish up this word or try to make it into something else, because if it comes out good it'll be right, but if it comes out bad it'll sound retarded,' and so in the middle of words that are over one syllable, I sometimes get confused and try to graft other words on top of them. Sometimes this makes good journalism and when they quote me it looks good in print, and other times it's very embarrassing. You can never predict what will come out when the words you're saying start to sound strange to you and you start to patch.

I really love English – like I love everything else that's American – it's just that I don't do that well with it. My hairdresser keeps telling me that learning foreign languages is good for business (he knows five, but then the little kids in Europe giggle when he talks, so I don't know how well he really knows them) and he tells me I should learn at least one, but I just can't. I can hardly talk what I already talk, so I don't want to branch out.

I admire people who do well with words, though, and I thought Truman Capote filled up space with words so well that when I first got to New York I began writing short fan letters to him and calling him on the phone every day until his mother told me to quit it.

I think a lot about 'space writers' – the writers who get paid by how much they write. I always think quantity is the best gauge on anything (because you're always doing the same thing, even if it looks like you're doing something else), so I set my sights on becoming a 'space artist'. When Picasso died I read in a magazine that he had made four thousand masterpieces in his lifetime and I thought, 'Gee, I could do that in a day.' So I started. And then I found out, 'Gee, it takes more than a day to do four thousand pictures.' You see, the way I do them, with my technique, I really thought I could do four thousand in a day. And they'd all be masterpieces because they'd all be the same painting. And I started and I got up to about five hundred and then I stopped. But it took more than a day, I think it took a month. So at five hundred a month, it would have taken me about eight months to do four thousand masterpieces – to be a 'space artist' and fill up spaces that I don't believe should be filled up anyway. It was disillusioning for me, to realize it would take me that long.

I like painting on a square because you don't have to decide whether it should be longer-longer or shorter-shorter or longer-shorter: it's just a square. I always wanted to do nothing but the same-size picture, but then somebody always comes along and says, 'You have to do it a little bit bigger,' or 'A little bit smaller.' You see, I think every painting should be the same size and the same color so they're all interchangeable and nobody thinks they have a better painting or a worse painting. And if the one 'master painting' is good, they're all good. Besides, even when the subject is different, people always paint the same painting.

When I have to think about it, I know the picture is wrong. And sizing is a form of thinking, and coloring is too. My instinct about painting says, 'If you don't think about it, it's right.' As soon as you have to decide and choose, it's wrong. And the more you decide about, the more wrong it gets. Some people, they paint abstract, so they sit there thinking about it because their thinking makes them feel they're doing something. But my thinking never makes me feel I'm doing anything. Leonardo da Vinci used to convince his patrons that his thinking time was worth something – worth even more than his painting time – and that may have been true for him, but I know that my thinking time isn't worth anything. I only expect to get paid for my 'doing' time.

When I paint:
I look at my canvas and I space it out right. I think, 'Well, over here in this corner it looks like it sort of belongs,' and so I say, 'Oh yes, that's where it belongs, all right.' So I look at it again and I say, 'The space in that corner there needs a little blue,' and so I put my blue up there and then, then I look over there and it looks blue over there so I take my brush and I move it over there and I make it blue over there, too. And then it needs to be more spaced, so I take my little blue brush and I blue it over there, and then I take my green brush and I put my green brush on it and I green it there, and then I walk back and I look at it and see if it's spaced right. And then – sometimes it's not spaced right – I take my colors and I put another little green over there and then if it's spaced right I leave it alone.

Usually, all I need is tracing paper and a good light. I can't understand why I was never an abstract expressionist, because with my shaking hand I would have been a natural.

I got a little into technology a couple of times. One of the times was when I thought it was the end of my art. I thought I was really really finished, so to mark the end of my art career I made silver pillows that you could just fill up with balloons and let fly away. I made them for a performance of the Merce Cunningham Dance Company. And then it turned out they didn't float away and we were stuck with them, so I guessed I wasn't really finished with art, since there I was, back again, putting anchors on the pillows. I had actually announced I was retiring from art. But then the Silver Space Pillows didn't float away and my career didn't float away, either. Incidentally, I've always said that silver was my favorite color because it reminded me of space, but now I'm thinking that over.

Another way to take up more space is with perfume.
I really love wearing perfume.
I'm not exactly a snob about the bottle a cologne comes in, but I am impressed with a good-looking presentation. It gives you confidence when you're picking up a well-designed bottle.

People have told me that the lighter your skin, the lighter the color perfume you should use. And vice-versa. But I can't limit myself to one range. (Besides, I'm sure hormones have a lot to do with how a perfume smells on your skin – I'm sure the right hormones can make Chanel No. 5 smell very butch.)

I switch perfumes all the time. If I've been wearing one perfume for three months, I force myself to give it up, even if I still feel like wearing it, so whenever I smell it again it will always remind me of those three months. I never go back to wearing it again; it becomes part of my permanent smell collection.

Sometimes at parties I slip away to the bathroom just to see what colognes they've got. I never look at anything else – I don't snoop – but I'm compulsive about seeing if there's some obscure perfume I haven't tried yet, or a good old favorite I haven't smelled in a long time. If I see something interesting, I can't stop myself from pouring it on. But then for the rest of the evening, I'm paranoid that the host or hostess will get a whiff of me and notice that I smell like somebody-they-know.

Of the five senses, smell has the closest thing to the full power of the past. Smell really is transporting. Seeing, hearing, touching, tasting are just not as powerful as smelling if you want your whole being to go back for a second to something. Usually I don't want to, but by having smells stopped up in bottles, I can be in control and can only smell the smells I want to, when I want to, to get the memories I'm in the mood to have. Just for a second. The good thing about a smell-memory is that the feeling

136

of being transported stops the instant you stop smelling, so there are no after-effects. It's a neat way to reminisce.

My collection of semi-used perfumes is very big by now, although I didn't start wearing lots of them until the early 60s. Before that the smells in my life were all just whatever happened to hit my nose by chance. But then I realized I had to have a kind of smell museum so certain smells wouldn't get lost forever. I loved the way the lobby of the Paramount Theater on Broadway used to smell. I would close my eyes and breathe deep whenever I was in it. Then they tore it down. I can look all I want at a picture of that lobby, but so what? I can't ever smell it again. Sometimes I picture a botany book in the future saying something like, 'The lilac is now extinct. Its fragrance is thought to have been similar to—?' and then what can they say? Maybe they'll be able to give it as a chemical formula. Maybe they already can.

I used to be afraid I would eventually run through and use up all the good colognes and there'd be nothing left but things like 'Grape' and 'Musk'. But now that I've been to the *profumerias* of Europe and seen all the colognes and perfumes they have there, I don't worry any more.

I get very excited when I read advertisements for perfume in the fashion magazines that were published in the 30s and 40s. I try to imagine from their names what they smelled like and I go crazy because I want to smell them all so much:

Guerlain's: 'Sous le Vent'
Lucien Le Long's : 'Jabot', 'Gardénia', 'Mon Image', 'Opening Night'
Prince Matchabelli's: 'Princess of Wales' in memory of Alexandra
Ciro's: 'Surrender', 'Réflexions'
Lenthéric's: ' Bientôt', 'Shanghai', 'Gardénia de Tahiti'
Worth's: 'Imprudence'
Marcel Rochas': 'Avenue Matignon', 'Air Jeune'
D'Orsay's: 'Trophée', 'Le Dandy', 'Toujours Fidèle', 'Belle de Jour'
Coty's: 'A Suma', 'La Fougeraie au Crépuscule' (Fernery at Twilight)

Corday's: 'Tzigane', 'Possession', 'Orchidée Bleue', 'Voyage à Paris'
Chanel's: brisk 'Cuir de Russie' (Russian Leather); romantic 'Glamour'; melting 'Jasmine'; tender 'Gardénia'
Molinelle's: 'Venez Voir'
Houbigant's: 'Countryclub', 'Demi-Jour' (Twilight)
Bonwit Teller's: '721'
Helena Rubinstein's: 'Town', 'Country'
Weil's: Eau de Cologne 'Carbonique'
Kathleen Mary Quinlan's: 'Rhythm'
Lengyel's (pronounced 'len-jel'): 'Impériale Russe'
Chevalier Garde's: 'H.R.R.', 'Fleur de Perse', 'Roi de Rome'
Saravel's: 'White Christmas'

When I'm walking around New York I'm always aware of the smells around me: the rubber mats in office buildings; upholstered seats in movie theaters; pizza; Orange Julius; espresso-garlic-oregano; burgers; dry cotton tee-shirts; neighborhood grocery stores; chic grocery stores; the hot dogs and sauerkraut carts; hardware store smell; stationery store smell; souvlaki; the leather and rugs at Dunhill, Mark Cross, Gucci; the Moroccan-tanned leather on the street-racks; new magazines, back-issue magazines; typewriter stores; Chinese import stores (the mildew from the freighter); India import stores; Japanese import stores; record stores; health food stores; soda-fountain drugstores; cut-rate drugstores; barber shops; beauty parlors; delicatessens; lumber yards; the wood chairs and tables in the N.Y. Public Library; the donuts, pretzels, gum, and grape soda in the subways; kitchen appliance departments; photo labs; shoe stores; bicycle stores; the paper and printing inks in Scribner's, Brentano's, Doubleday's, Rizzoli, Marboro, Bookmasters, Barnes & Noble; shoe-shine stands; grease-batter; hair pomade; the good cheap candy smell in the front of Woolworth's and the dry-goods smell in the back; the horses by the Plaza Hotel; bus and truck exhaust; architects' blueprints; cumin, fenu-greek, soy sauce, cinnamon; fried platanos; the

train tracks in Grand Central Station; the banana smell of dry
cleaners; exhausts from apartment house laundry rooms; East
Side bars (creams); West Side bars (sweat); newspaper stands;
record stores; fruit stands in all the different seasons – strawberry,
watermelon, plum, peach, kiwi, cherry, Concord grape, tangerine,
murcot, pineapple, apple – and I love the way the smell of each
fruit gets into the rough wood of the crates and into the
tissue-paper wrappings.

I know from experience that I prefer city space to country space.
I love the idea of being in the country, but then when I get there
it comes back to me that:

I love to walk but I can't
I love to swim but I can't
I love to sit in the sun but I can't
I love to smell the flowers but I can't
I love to play tennis but I can't
I love to water-ski but I can't

The list could run longer, but that's the idea, and the reason 'I
can't' is simply because I'm *not the type*. You just can't do things
that you're not the type to do. You can *say things* that you're not
the type to say, but you can't *do things* that you're not the type
to do. It's a bad idea.

Also, when I'm in the country, I love to watch television but I
can't, because the reception is usually too bad.

(By the way, people will often try to convince you to do
something by saying that it doesn't matter if you're not the type,
or that you could be the type if you wanted to be, but don't
break down and try to do something that you're not the type to
do, because you know what type you are, nobody else does.)

I'm a city boy. In the big cities they've set it up so you can go to
a park and be in a miniature countryside, but in the countryside
they don't have any patches of big city, so I get very homesick.

Another reason I like the city better than the country is that
in the city everything is geared to working, and in the country
everything is geared to relaxation. I like working better than

relaxing. In the city, even the trees in the parks work hard because the number of people they have to make oxygen and chlorophyll for is staggering. If you lived in Canada you might have a million trees making oxygen for you alone, so each of those trees isn't working that hard. Whereas a tree in a treepot in Times Square has to make oxygen for a million people. In New York you really do have to hustle, and the trees know this, too – just look at them. The other day on 57th Street, I was walking and I was looking at the new, sloping Solow building across the street and I walked straight into a treepot. I was embarrassed because there was no way at all to carry it off. I just fell on top of this tree on West 57th Street because I wasn't ready for it to be there.

Somehow, the way life works, people usually wind up either in crowded subways and elevators, or in big rooms all by themselves. Everybody should have a big room they can go to and everybody should also ride the crowded subways.

Usually people are very tired when they ride on a subway, so they can't sing and dance, but I think if they could sing and dance on a subway, they'd really enjoy it.

The kids who spray graffiti all over the subway cars at night have learned how to recycle city space very well. They go back into the subway yards in the middle of the night when the cars are empty and that's when they do their singing and their dancing on the subway. The subways are like palaces at night with all that space just for you.

Ghetto space is wrong for America. It's wrong for people who are the same type to go and live together. There shouldn't be any huddling together in the same groups with the same food. In America it's got to mix 'n' mingle. If I were President, I'd make people mix 'n' mingle more. But the thing is America's a free country and I couldn't make them.

I believe in living in one room. One empty room with just a bed, a tray, and a suitcase. You can do everything either from your bed or in your bed – eat, sleep, think, get exercise, smoke – and

140

you would have a bathroom and a telephone right next to the bed.

Everything is more glamorous when you do it in bed, anyway. Even peeling potatoes.

Suitcase space is so efficient. A suitcase full of everything you need:

One spoon
One fork
One plate
One cup

One shirt
One underwear
One sock
One shoe

One suitcase and one empty room. Terrific. Perfect.

By living in one room you eliminate a lot of worries. But the basic worries, unfortunately, remain:

Are the lights on or off?
Is the water off?
Are the cigarettes out?
Is the back door closed?
Is the elevator working?
Is there anyone in the lobby?
Who's that sitting in my lap?

People are sleeping in pyramid-shaped spaces a lot now because they think it will keep them young and vital and stop the aging process. I'm not worried about that because I have my wings. However, my ideal too is the pyramid-look, because you don't have to think about a ceiling. You want to have a roof over your head, so why not let your walls also be your ceiling, so you have one less thing to think about – one less surface to look at, one less surface to clean, one less surface to paint. The tepee-dwelling Indians had the right idea. A cone might be nice if circles didn't exclude the edges and if you could find the right round sink, but I prefer an equilateral-triangular pyramidal-shaped enclosure even more than a square-based pyramid shape, because with a triangular base you have one less wall to think about, and one less corner to dust.

My ideal city would be one long Main Street with no cross streets or side streets to jam up traffic. Just one long one-way street. With one tall vertical building where everybody lived with:

One elevator
One doorman
One mailbox
One washing machine
One garbage can
One tree out front
One movie theater next door

Main Street would be very very wide, and all you'd have to say to someone to make them feel good is, 'I saw you on Main Street today.'

And you'd fill your car up with gas and drive across the street.

My ideal city would be completely new. *No antiques*. All the buildings would be new. Old buildings are unnatural spaces. Buildings should be built to last for a short time. And if they're older than ten years, I say get rid of them. I'd build new buildings every fourteen years. The building and the tearing down would keep people busy, and the water wouldn't be rusty from old pipes.

Rome, Italy, is an example of what happens when the buildings in a city last too long.

They call Rome 'The Eternal City' because everything is so old and everything is still standing. They always say, 'Rome wasn't built in a day.' Well, I say maybe it should have been, because the quicker you build something, the shorter a time it lasts, and the shorter a time it lasts, the sooner people have jobs again, replacing it. Replacing necessities keeps people busy. The necessities, they always say, are food, shelter, and clothing. Now, in Italy they make a lot of food, and they make a lot of clothing, but food and clothing are only two-thirds of the necessities, the other third is shelter — and they're not making that because it's already been made. So what's happened in Rome is that the women wind up in the kitchens making all the food and in the factories sewing all the clothes, while the men don't do anything because the buildings are already built and they're not falling down! Their buildings were originally built too well and they've never corrected the situation. This is why you see so many men on the streets of Rome, Italy, at all hours of the day and night.

The best, most temporal way of making a building that I ever heard of is by making it with light. The Fascists did a lot of this 'light architecture'. If you build buildings with lights outside, you can make them indefinite, and then when you're through using them you shut the lights off and they disappear. Hitler always needed buildings in a hurry to make speeches from, so his architect created these 'buildings' for him that were illusion buildings, completely constructed by lighting effects, where he defined a very big space.

Holograms are going to be exciting, I think. You can really, finally, with holograms, pick your own atmosphere. They'll be televising a party, and you want to be there, and with holograms, you will be there. You'll be able to have this 3-D party in your house, you'll be able to pretend you're there and walk in with the people. You can even rent a party. You can have anybody famous that you want sitting right next to you.

I like to be the right thing in the wrong space and the wrong thing in the right space. But when you hit one of the two, people turn the lights out on you, or spit on you, or write bad reviews of you, or beat you up, or mug you, or say you're 'climbing'. But usually being the right thing in the wrong space and the wrong thing in the right space is worth it, because something funny always happens. Believe me, because I've made a career out of being the right thing in the wrong space and the wrong thing in the right space. That's one thing I really do know about.

When people have a cool, calm atmosphere about them, they're usually spaced. They have those right kind of eyes, and they sit around and not bother anybody. Some people are like that naturally because of their chemicals, and other people are like that because of drugs. They think they're thinking – about something.

Energy helps you fill up more space, but if I had more energy than usual, I'd probably not want to fill up more space – I'd be in my room cleaning a lot. I'll say this for diet pills: they make you think small, and when you think small, you do a lot of cleaning up. Real energy makes you want to run down the beach doing cartwheels even if you can't do them. But diet-pill energy helps you fill up less space because it makes you want to recopy address books while you *talk* for an hour about running down the beach doing cartwheels. Diet pills make you want to dust and flush things down the john.

In New York you have to clean so much, and when you're finished, it's not-dirty. In Europe people clean so much, and when they're finished, it's not just not-dirty, it's clean. Also, it seems so much easier to entertain in Europe than in New York. You just throw open the doors to the garden and eat out in the open air with flowers and trees all around. Whereas New York is funny, most of the time things just don't come off. In Europe, even having tea in the back yard can be wonderful. But in New York it's complicated – if the restaurant is nice, the food can be bad and if the food is good, the lighting can be bad, and if the lighting is good, the air circulation can be bad.

And New York restaurants now have a new thing – they don't sell their food, they sell their atmosphere. They say, 'How dare you say we don't have good food, when we never said we had good food. We have good *atmosphere*.' They caught on that what people really care about is changing their atmosphere for a couple of hours. That's why they can get away with just selling their atmosphere with a minimum of actual food. Pretty soon when food prices go really up, they'll be selling only atmosphere. If people are really all that hungry, they can bring food with them when they go out to dinner, but otherwise, instead of 'going out to dinner' they'll just be 'going out to atmosphere'.

My favorite restaurant atmosphere has always been the atmosphere of the good, plain, American lunchroom or even the good plain American lunchcounter. The old-style Schrafft's and the old-style Chock Full O' Nuts are absolutely the only things in the world that I'm truly nostalgic for. The days were carefree in the 1940s and 1950s when I could go into a Chocks for my cream cheese sandwich with nuts on date-nut bread and not worry about a thing. No matter what changes or how fast, the one thing we all always need is real good food so we can know what the changes are and how fast they're coming. Progress is very important and exciting in everything except food. When you say you want an orange, you don't want someone asking you, 'An orange what?'

I really like to eat alone. I want to start a chain of restaurants for other people who are like me called ANDY-MATS – 'The Restaurant for the Lonely Person'. You get your food and then you take your tray into a booth and watch television.

Today my favorite kind of atmosphere is the airport atmosphere. If I didn't have to think about the idea that airplanes go up in the air and fly it would be my perfect atmosphere. Airplanes and airports have my favorite kind of food service, my favorite kind of bathrooms, my favorite peppermint Life Savers, my favorite kinds of entertainment, my favorite loudspeaker address systems, my favorite conveyor belts, my favorite graphics and colors, the best security checks, the best views, the best perfume shops, the best employees, and the best optimism. I love the way you don't have to think about where you're going, someone else is doing that, but I just can't get over the crazy feeling I get when I look out and see the clouds and know I'm really up-there. The atmosphere is great, it's the idea of flying that I question. I guess

I'm not an air person, but I'm on an air schedule, so I have to live an air life. I'm embarrassed that I don't like to fly because I love to be modern, but I compensate by loving airports and airplanes so much.

The best atmosphere I can think of is film, because it's three-dimensional physically and two-dimensional emotionally.

|| Success

B Is it raining?
A I think they're spitting at us.

B and I spent the afternoon sitting on a couch in the lobby of the Grand Hotel in Rome, watching the Stars and their hairdressers go up and down the marble staircase. It was just like watching a play.

I'd been flown to Rome for an Event that evening which had pulled a lot of big stars into town. We were celebrity-spotting. B compared us to Lucy Ricardo and Ethel Mertz in the lobby of the Beverly Hills. I'd been saying for years that Rome is the new celebrity center, the new Hollywood.

B was feeling very grand. 'This means you've really made it,' he said, 'when they fly you in and we can sit around all day in a glamorous lobby like this, watching everybody we've ever seen in every magazine and every movie . . .'

At that moment I was more impressed with the couch than I was with the stars on the stairs. The tireder you are, the less impressed you are. With anything. If I'd gotten some sleep on the plane I might have been excited too.

'We've sat in hotel lobbies all over New York and all over the world, and it's always nice,' I said. The lobbies are always the best-looking place in the hotel – you wish you could bring out a cot and sleep in them. Compared to the lobby, your room always looks like a closet.

'No,' B said, 'but there's something about traveling thousands of miles—'

'—to sit in a lobby.'

'—of traveling thousands of miles to sit in a place like this. If it were just down the block I wouldn't think it was that great, but the fact that we came all this way makes it exciting.'

I told B that if it weren't for the plane ordeal I'd like to be in Europe one day a week. But somehow I can't be one of those people who doesn't think about what it means to be up there and flying. Airports and airplanes have my favorite kind of food, my favorite kind of bathroom, my favorite kind of nonservile service, my favorite peppermint Life Savers, my favorite kinds of entertainment, my favorite kind of lack of responsibility for your own direction, my favorite shops, my favorite graphics – my favorite everything. I even love the security checks. But I just can't get over hating to fly.

'Just think of all the exciting things you're missing,' B said.

Actually, I jade very quickly. Once is usually enough. Either *once only*, or *every day*. If you do something once it's exciting, and if you do it every day it's exciting. But if you do it, say, twice or just almost every day, it's not good any more. Nothing in-between is as good as once or every day.

A tall handsome man walked into the lobby from outside. He was wearing red slacks and a red shirt with a white patent belt and matching espadrilles. He was Liz Taylor's hairdresser.

'He likes red,' B noted.

'He looks good in red. He looks different than he did the last time. I guess he's lost weight,' I said, trying to pin-point the Improvement. 'Let's tell him.'

'Here comes Franco,' said B. 'He's always scratching his balls, do you think he has crabs?'

'No, he's just Italian.' Franco Rossellini was our host for the Event that night and had taken care of all the details for travel and accommodations. Franco has a way of being always solicitous and at the same time totally distracted. He asked us if everything was okay with our tickets and our room, while his eyes darted around the lobby looking for signs of Liz. I asked him if he could pull some strings and get us rooms for a few additional days because we had to stay on after the Event to do some business art. We were having trouble getting an extension because there was an Other Event happening two days after the Event, so our rooms were only reserved for us for the following day and after that we were on our own. When Franco realized what 'pull a few strings' meant he got dramatic:

'Do you know they called me for a room for Elizabeth Taylor

because there is not even a room for her! And it takes her two days to unpack! With the Other Event coming in, everything is a disaster!'

Just then a Milanese journalist wandered by and asked me how I liked Rome.

Well, I really like Rome because it's a kind of museum the way Bloomingdale's is a kind of museum, but I was too tired to talk that way. Besides, he seemed nice, but almost every journalist never wants to know what you really think – they just want the answers that fit the questions that fit the story they want to write, and their idea usually is that you shouldn't let your own personality butt in on the article they're writing about you or else they'll really hate you for sure for giving them more work, because the more answers you give, the more answers they have to twist to fit their story. So it's better just to smile and say you like Rome and let them give their reasons that they have for you to like it. And anyway, I was tired. I was glad to see Franco coming back over. He always breaks up tension.

'I'm back,' he announced. 'I've just been posing for the *paparazzi*. I shouldn't do that.'

I told Franco that B had fallen in love in Bulgari's with a girl behind a diamond display who he said looked like Dominique Sanda. Franco understands about 'love' and knew the symptoms: 'So now are you running into the store all of the time buying all of Bulgari? That's expensive. You should fall in love with a waitress; that's not so expensive.'

'It's not expensive because I'm not buying anything. I'm just going in and out, in and out,' said B.

Franco made himself world-weary long enough to say, 'In-and-out in-and-out . . . What else is there to do . . .' Then he rushed off to talk to some director.

B spotted Liz Taylor walking on the other side of the lobby and tried to make me paranoid by suggesting that she was avoiding me. I could see her out of the corner of my eye.

Then Sergio, one of Franco's assistants, came up and asked B if I could be ready a half hour early so I could go with Liz to meet

Princess Grace so we could all walk into the Event together. That was the plan. B was jealous that he wasn't going with us, so as soon as Sergio walked away he said, 'He says that like it's so important. He's so used to dealing with Liz through her hairdresser that he thinks he has to talk to you through me, even when you're standing right here.'

I told B that what we should have bought him in Bulgari's was a big gold comb. 'You should have a giant hairdresser's gold comb. The kind of comb they use for teasing. In gold.' B and I laughed about our *faux pas* in going into Bulgari's and asking for something in silver. We were so nervous because they had us sit down, and then there was nothing to look at – we didn't know what to do with our eyes – and we didn't want to say that we wanted the cheapest thing they had, so B had thought quickly and asked for a swizzle stick in silver, and the girl he was in love with said, 'I'm sorry, we have nothing in silver here,' so love went down the drain.

'Love went down the drain,' agreed B. 'I didn't like her any more after she said that anyway. And up close she didn't look that much like Dominique Sanda.'

Just then B and I both heard a hissing noise from a corner of the lobby, and B told me not to get paranoid, that it was just a waxing machine. He asked me what I'd do if I got hissed at the Event that night. I told him that I'd been hissed before. He asked me when that was and I told him about getting hissed on college tours.

Then a horrible thought occurred to me – what if I was expected to make a speech at the Event. After all, it was a very official Event, and a benefit yet, and usually at benefits they have speeches.

B decided that we should write a speech right now just in case. We decided I would get up and say what a great thrill and honor it was to work with Liz Taylor's hairdressers – 'Let's hear it for Ramon and Gianni!' And then I'd ask Liz to introduce B—I'd say, 'Liz Taylor has changed my life: now I, too, have my own hairdressers. I've taken my business manager and my photographer and my redactor and my social secretary and made them all hairdressers.'

Elsa Martinelli came by to ask us if we were wearing black jackets or white jackets tonight because her husband Willy had forgotten his black one and wondered if a white one would be all right, because he didn't want to be the only one in a white jacket or else people would be mistaking him for a waiter and asking him for drinks. B said that the best he could do would be to wear his white pants because he didn't have a white jacket, and Elsa thought that that would make Willy feel better. B asked Elsa what her tee-shirt had embroidered on it. Her explanation was something like:

'Oh, this is a crazy Neapolitan thing. He doesn't know how to speak English very well, so for him – the designer – this means, 47, that's forty – means "fuck" in Neapolitan – seven—'

Christian De Sica tapped Elsa on the shoulder and they went into the restaurant.

'*Ciao.*'

'*Ciao.*'

We were quiet for a few minutes, and I started to think about face images. B asked me what I was thinking about and I told him I was thinking about 'portraits'.

The waxing machine was on our side of the lobby now. 'Poptarts?' B asked. You see, he couldn't hear.

I liked that. 'Yes. Poptarts. It's funny because if someone gets a poptart when they're old, then is the artist supposed to make them look "younger"? It's really hard to know. I've seen poptarts done by famous artists who painted old people looking old. So then, should you have your poptart done when you're very young so that will be the image that's left? But that would be strange, too . . .'

This B's idea of a wonderful date would be to take out the most eccentric, most rich, most old lady he could find, so he was in favor of Age before Beauty. 'A person's personality doesn't show in their face until they're old. There's something about the force of a personality that comes through. So a "poptart" should be flattering, in the sense that it's a reflection of a positive part of the person's personality.'

Just then Ursula Andress appeared at the top of the stairs. She looked beautiful. She was talking to her hairdresser. I could tell that they were talking about her hair. He was making gestures around it as if he were giving ideas. It was a very glamorous scene.

B and I started to argue over how tall she was. I said she was short and B said she wasn't so short.

B said, 'She looks great. She doesn't look short.'

I said, 'No. She's very short.'

B said, 'But she doesn't look short.'

I said, 'She has shoes on.'

B said, 'She has underarm perspiration. Look! She's smelling under her arms!'

I said, 'That's right, but she's smart not to use deodorant because it's poison, and also you never know when you're really nervous. She's smart to want to know when she's nervous.'

B said, 'She still doesn't look short to me.'

I said, 'I know she doesn't look it. I didn't used to think she was so short either until I saw pictures of her.'

B screamed, 'BUT YOU'RE LOOKING AT THE ACTUAL GIRL! DOES SHE *LOOK* SHORT TO YOU?'

I said, 'She's standing next to her hairdresser, and her hairdresser's short too, so you can't tell.'

She started down the staircase.

I said, 'Look, she's two steps up from him and she's not staring down at him! Come on, B, admit it, she's a peanut!'

B wouldn't admit it. 'All right,' he said, 'she's not tall, but she's not a peanut.'

I said, 'I bet she's even shorter than I think. I bet she has those big high shoes on. We can't see them because her pants come right down to the rug, but I bet she has four-inch clogs on.'

B said, 'But her look is so long. She's certainly not as short as some people.'

'Yes she is,' I said. 'She's shorter.'

B started to go crazy. 'YOU'RE DETERMINED TO BELIEVE SHE'S A PEANUT!'

154

I said, 'I MET HER, B! YOU MET HER TOO! YOU KNOW HOW SHORT SHE IS!'

'SHE WAS SITTING DOWN!'

'No,' I said softly, 'she got up.'

'She wasn't that short.' This B was stubborn. He said it in a final way, as if now that was that.

I said in an even more final way, 'She's a peanut.' I stared at B. He was tired of arguing. I'd won.

Then while his defenses were down I said. 'Look, if you were doing your job you would have gone over there and asked her for an interview.'

'What should I do, run over and interview her on how it feels to be the shortest woman in the world???'

'Well, she *is* short . . .' I said. 'There's no getting away from that.'

Ursula came down another step and B started up again, 'Look, she just came down a step and you can see her heels and they're not that high. She's got short heels on. She's actually quite tall.'

I said, 'B . . . Next to that guy she's tall, because he's a bigger peanut than she is. Don't worry, B – Liz Taylor is also very short. All the great stars are short!'

B started laughing. 'But Liz is shaped like that blue vase over there, with her hair being the flowers and her hips being the table . . .'

I said, 'You know, B, one of these days Liz will pay attention to you or say something nice to you, and you'll end up really liking her.'

B said, 'I do like her, but she *is* shaped like that vase, and her hair *is* like those flowers in it.'

'B, she'll come up to me someday and say, "I hear you have the best hairdresser in the world," and then she'll look at you and say, "How would you like to work for me? And take ten per cent of everything I make." '

I yawned. 'I feel like two old ladies,' I told B.

B said, 'Oh this is too much under one roof – Liz, Paulette, Ursula, Elsa, Sylvie, Marina Cicogna, Sao Schlumberger . . .'

'You're naming off the biggest stars in the world, B. And don't forget Mrs Rochas.'

B went on, '. . . Mrs Rochas, Christina Ford, Betty Catroux, Guido Mannari – all in one room. Christian De Sica . . .'

'Oh,' I said, 'he's adorable. Is it okay for guys to be adorable?'

'It's okay for anybody to be adorable,' B said.

My wife was running low and I was tired: time to go up to my room and snooze before getting dressed for the Event.

12 **Art**

A You take some chocolate . . . and you take two pieces of
bread . . . and you put the candy in the middle and you make
a sandwich of it. And that would be cake.

We were staying at the Hotel Mirabeau in Monte Carlo in a suite lent us by friends after we were asked to vacate the nearby Hotel de Paris because B had forgotten to extend our reservations in advance for the grand Grand Prix week-end. My room overlooked a hairpin curve of the racetrack. I could see – and I could definitely hear – all the Grand Prix preliminaries from the moment they began at five-thirty every morning and as they continued throughout the day.

I was organizing some transcripts when B and Damian knocked on the door to see if I was ready to go out for lunch. They were early. Damian looked beautiful in a navy-blue Dior. When you asked her out, you never knew in advance if she'd look like a million or like two cents. And the way she'd decide she should look would have nothing to do with where you were going – she might wear a Valentino to a rock concert and jeans to a Halston party. In fact, that's probably exactly what she would wear to both.

Damian and B held their ears when they heard the noise. 'I was thinking about racing,' said B as twenty little cars with big engines roared by. 'Any minute those cars could go right over.'

'I think it's just to see who can make the most noise,' I said.

'Do you think the drivers have death wishes?'

I said, 'I just think they want to make a Big Splash. Like when Andrea "Whips" Feldman jumped out the window and said she was "going for the Big Time: Heaven." I don't think they think about death – it's more the idea of the Big Time.'

'Then why don't they try to become movie stars?'

'That would be a come-down,' I explained, 'because all the movie stars are trying to become race-car drivers. And besides, all the new movie stars are the sports people – they're the really

159

good-looking people, the exciting people – and they make the most money.'

The roar died down as the cars sped across to the other side of town. Now it sounded more like a 707 than an Apollo lift-off. I tried to enjoy the relative silence for a minute, because in another minute they'd be back – it only took that long to run the course. B remembered a phone call he had to make and went back to his room to talk where it was less noisy.

Damian and I were alone in the room now and if my wife weren't there, too, I would have panicked. I used to always panic when I was alone with people – I mean, without a B – until I got my wife.

Damian walked over to the window and looked out. 'I guess you have to take a lot of risks to be famous in any field,' she said, and then, turning around to look at me, she added: 'For instance, to be an artist.'

She was being so serious, but it was just like a bad movie. I love bad movies. I was starting to remember why I always liked Damian.

I gestured toward the gift-wrapped salami that was sticking out of my Pan Am flight bag and said, 'Any time you slice a salami, you take a risk.'

'No, but I mean for an artist—'

'An artist!!' I interrupted. 'What do you mean, an "artist"? An artist can slice a salami, too! Why do people think artists are special? It's just another job.'

Damian wouldn't let me disillusion her. Some people have deep-rooted long-standing art fantasies. I remembered a freezing winter night a couple of years ago when I was dropping her off at two-thirty in the morning after a very social party and she made me take her to Times Square to find a record store that was open so she could buy *Blonde on Blonde* and get back in touch with 'real people'. Some people have deep-rooted long-standing art fantasies and they really stick with them.

'But to become a famous artist you had to do something that was "different". And if it was "different", then it means you

160

took a risk, because the critics could have said that it was bad instead of good.'

'In the first place,' I said, 'they usually did say it was bad. And in the second place, if you say that artists take "risks", it's insulting to the men who landed on D-Day, to stunt men, to baby-sitters, to Evel Knievel, to stepdaughters, to coal miners, and to hitch-hikers, because they're the ones who really know what "risks" are.' She didn't even hear me, she was still thinking about what glamorous 'risks' artists take.

'They always say new art is bad for a while, and that's the risk – that's the pain you have to have for fame.'

I asked her how she could say 'new art'. 'How do you know if it's new or not? New art's never new when it's done.'

'Oh yes it is. It has a new look that your eyes can't adjust to at first.'

I waited for the cars to roar around the hairpin curve again below my window. The building was shaking slightly. I wondered what was taking B so long.

'No,' I said. 'It's not new art. You don't know it's new. You don't know *what* it is. It doesn't become new until about ten years later, because then it looks new.'

'So what's new right now?' she asked. I couldn't think of anything so I said I didn't want to commit myself.

'Is what's new now what happened ten years ago?'

That was pretty smart. I said, 'MMmmmmaybe.'

'That's what that lesbian was saying at lunch. She said that even the very intelligent French people who are interested in everything cultural don't know the names of famous American modern artists. They're just now learning about Jasper Johns and Rauschenberg. But what I want to know is, when people were saying how bad your movies and art were, did it bother you? Did it hurt to open the newspapers and read how bad your work was?'

'No.'

'It didn't bother you when a critic said you couldn't paint?'

'I never read the paper,' I said. It was lift-off time again.

'That's not true,' she yelled, miraculously making herself heard above the noise. 'I see you reading the papers all the time.' She looked around the room at the piles of newspapers and magazines. 'You *buy* enough of them.'

'I look at the pictures, that's all.'

'Come off it. I've heard you make comments after reading your reviews.'

Well, I never used to read the papers, especially reviews of my own work. But now I read very carefully every review of everything that I produce – that is, everything that has my name on it.

'When I used to do the work myself,' I explained to Damian, 'I never read any reviews or any of my own publicity. But then when I sort of stopped *doing* things and started *producing* things, I did want to know what people were saying about them because it wouldn't be anything personal. It was a business decision that I made to start reading reviews of the things I produced, because as the head of a company, I felt that I had other people to think about. So I also constantly think of new ways to present the same thing to interviewers, which is another reason I now read the reviews – I go through them and see if anybody says anything to us or about us we can use. Like today in this French paper the writer called my tape recorder such a great name – a "magnetophone".'

I went over to the pile of newspapers and found the article I was talking about. 'Doesn't that look nice on the page? Different. A new word for the same thing.'

'Did you read the review of yourself in the Liz Taylor movie?'

'Of course not, because that's something I did myself so I don't want to know what anybody thinks about it. I told B to tear it out of the paper before he gave it to me.'

'It said you were "slightly repellent, like a reptile".'

She was testing me to see if it really didn't bother me when I heard things like that about myself. It really didn't. I didn't even know what it meant to be 'like a reptile'. 'Does that mean I'm slimy?' I asked her.

'There's something about reptiles,' she said. 'Looks aside. They're the only animals who don't like to be touched.' As she said that she jumped out of the chair. 'You don't mind being touched, do you?' She was coming at me.

'Yes! Yes I do!' She kept coming. I didn't know how to stop her. I panicked and screamed, 'You're fired!' but it didn't do any good because she didn't work for me. That's one reason I only like to be with Bs who work for me. She put her pinky on my elbow and I screamed, 'Get your hands off me, Damian!'

She shrugged and said, 'Can't say I didn't try.' She walked back into her corner. 'You do hate it when people touch you. I remember when I first met you, I bumped into you and you jumped about six feet. Why is that? Afraid of germs?'

'No. Afraid of getting attacked.'

'Did you get this way after you were shot?'

'I was always like this. I always try to have a corner of my eye open. I always look behind me, above me.' Then I corrected myself – 'Not always. Usually I forget, but I mean to.'

I walked over to the window. We were fourteen stories up. This was the highest I'd ever slept. Not the highest above sea level, but the highest up in a building. I always talk about how I'd love to live on the top floor of a high rise, but then I get next to a window and I just can't handle it. I'm always afraid of rolling right out. The windows here went down so close to the floor that I'd rolled the metal shutters down the night before. I don't understand the idea rich people have of living higher and higher. I knew a couple in Chicago who lived in one high-rise building and then when a higher rise was built next door they moved into that one. I walked away from the window. Maybe my fear of being up high is chemical.

I always bring every problem back to chemicals, because I really think that everything starts and finishes with chemicals.

'You mean you don't get wiser as you grow up?' B said as he walked back into the room.

'Yes,' I said. 'You do. You have to, so you usually do.'

B said, 'But if you know what it's all about, you get discouraged and you don't want to live.'

'You don't?' I said.

'Right.' Damian agreed with B. 'If you're wiser it doesn't make you happier. One of the girls in one of your movies said something like "I don't want to be smart, because being smart makes you depressed." '

She was quoting Geri Miller in *Flesh*. Being smart could make you depressed, certainly, if you weren't smart about what you were smart about. It's viewpoint that's important – not intelligence, probably.

'You're saying that you're wiser this year than you were last year?' B asked me.

I was, so I said, 'Yes.'

'How? What did you learn this year that you didn't know before?'

'Nothing. That's why I'm wiser. That extra year of learning more nothing.'

B laughed. Damian didn't.

'I don't understand,' she said. 'If you keep learning more nothing, that makes it harder and harder to live.'

Learning about nothing doesn't make it harder, it makes it easier, but most people make Damian's mistake of thinking it makes it harder. That's a big mistake.

She said, 'If you know life is nothing, then what are you living for?'

'For nothing.'

'But I love being a woman. That's not nothing,' she said.

'Being a woman is just as nothing as being a man. Either way you have to shave and that's a big nothing. Right?' I was oversimplifying, but it was true.

Damian laughed. 'Then why do you keep on making paintings? They're going to hang around after you die.'

'That's nothing,' I said.

'It's an *idea* that goes on,' she insisted.

'Ideas are nothing.'

164

B suddenly got a crafty look on his face. 'Okay, okay. We agree. Then the only purpose in life is—'

'Nothing.' I cut him off.

But it didn't stop him. '—to have as much fun as possible.' Now I knew what he was trying to do. He was hinting for me to hand them some cash for 'expenses' that afternoon.

'If ideas are nothing,' B continued, laying his argument for easy money, 'and objects are nothing, then as soon as you get some money you should just spend it having as good a time as possible.'

'Well,' I said, 'it doesn't mean if you don't believe in nothing that it's nothing. You have to treat the nothing as if it were something. Make something out of nothing.' That threw him off the track.

'What???'

I repeated myself word for word, which was hard. 'It doesn't mean if you don't believe in nothing that it's nothing.' The dollar signs slipped out of B's eyes. It's always good to get abstract when it comes to economics.

'Okay, say I believe in nothing,' Damian said. 'How would I convince myself to become an actress or write a novel? The only way I could ever write a novel would be because I believed it was really going to be something, to have this book with my name on it, or to become a famous actress.'

'You can become a nothing actress,' I told her, 'and if you really believe in nothing you can write a book about it.'

'But then to get famous you have to write a book about something people care about. A, you just can't say that everything is nothing!' Now she was getting upset, but she kept thinking, trying to come up with a way to make me say that something was something.

I repeated, 'Everything is nothing.'

'Okay,' she said, 'say I agree with you. Then sex would be nothing!'

'Sex is nothing, right. Absolutely correct.'

'But it's not! Why would people want it so much if it's nothing!'

Everybody has to come to their own conclusions about sex – it's not something you can convince them with by argument. But just for the exercise I said, 'What happens when you have sex, Damian?'

She thought about it for a second and said, 'I don't know, it's nice, you feel the other person's body, your emotions somehow get involved, I don't know, you just feel different than you do the rest of the time.'

'And then you come,' I said.

'And then you come, okay. But you feel different, even if you don't come. It feels natural and normal. And different – afterwards if I think back on it I can't believe I did it!' She laughed.

'Look,' I said. 'Say you think that it was really something and the person you had sex with thinks that it was nothing.'

Damian looked hurt now. I realized that she was taking my hypothetical case personally. 'Well, if that person thought it was so nothing, why would he want to sleep with me again?'

'Because,' I explained, 'he thought it was nothing and you thought it was something, that's why. That's the reason you're doing it again. He likes to do nothing and you like to do something.'

B said, 'So it all comes down to what a person thinks: in other words, there's nothing objective, really. It's all subjective. I could say, "Wasn't that something that we did today?" and the other person would say what they thought, but it actually was the same thing happening – the same lips kissed the same lips. A camera would show it just the same, no matter what you thought.'

'Show what?' My mind always drifts when I hear words like 'objective' and 'subjective' – I never know what people are talking about, I just don't have the brains. 'Show what?' I asked again.

'Two people kissing.'

'Two people kissing,' I said, 'always look like they're fish. Two people kissing, what does it mean, anyway?'

Damian said, 'It means you trust the other person enough to let them touch you.'

166

'No it doesn't. People kiss people they don't trust all the time. Especially in Europe and at parties. Think of all the people we know who'll kiss anybody. Does that mean they're "trusting"?'

'I think it does, yes.' B said. This B was stubborn. 'They trust a lot of people, is all.'

B kissed Damian. Two people kissing always look like fish.

13 Titles

I woke up in my hotel room in Torino a little later than usual, and I went through the standard away-from-home one-second-panic of wondering where I was. I was pretty tired from hopping around Europe chasing after my hairdresser trying to consummate the business art deals he set up. I was at the Grand Excelsior Principi di Savoia Hotel. The Grand Excelsior Principi di Savoia Hotel was the only first-class hotel in town, probably because there were no first-class names left over for any others.

I had come to Torino on art business, but I wished I were there to do some business art – Torino is where Fiats are made. I half-recalled eating a lot of Italian nougats once that were made in Torino, so I started wishing I were there to be photographed for a big billboard advertisement for Fiat or Perugia candy. For some reason, billboard ads are more striking in Italy than anywhere else. The Italians really know how to put out good billboards.

Italian television is something else, however, and as soon as it sunk in that I wouldn't be watching Barbara Walters, Pat Collins, or 'Make Room For Daddy', I reached for the phone to ring B's room to wake him up so he could call room service for breakfast, because I'm too insecure to make the call myself.

I really torture the people I travel with. When I'm traveling I'm as demanding as Liz Taylor or Madame Helena Rubinstein (was). The people – the Bs – I travel with have to act as interpreter/buffers between me and the entire culture I'm in, and they also have to entertain me constantly in some way, because I go nuts without American television. The people I travel with have to be very good-natured and easy-going in order to take what I put them through without cracking themselves, because they have to somehow get us home.

'Wake up, B, it's nine-thirty.'

This B groaned, but it sounded like a fairly good-natured groan. I told him to order breakfast and we could have a party in my room. Then I took the fall from the bed to the floor – it really was a high bed – and I strolled to the bathroom.

In a few minutes there was a knock at the door and B stumbled in, followed, more steadily, by room service – a dark-eyed blonde with a bowl of cherries floating in ice-cold water, dry toast, tea, and coffee. I handed B a tip to hand to her.

'*Molto grazie.*'

'*Ciao, bella.*' B was leching.

'*Grazie, signor.*' She was blushing. '*Ciao.*'

'The Torinese are so beautiful,' said B, sitting down to breakfast after she left. 'The best of North and South.'

I was already on my tenth cherry. They were big and firm and deep red and ice-cold.

'So B,' I asked, 'are we having a good time so far, do you think? Is it exciting at all?'

'The question is,' corrected B, 'is your wife having a good time.'

My wife. The tape recorder.

'Oh right. My wife . . . Not really, no. Queen Soraya made me shut her off.'

'I heard her tell you to and then somebody said you looked so sad sitting next to Soraya, and I said, "Oh it's just because she made him turn off his tape. A likes everybody except people who make him turn off his tape. It's like saying come to dinner but don't bring your wife." '

I was on my twentieth consecutive cherry. I asked B if it didn't feel nice for him to be back in the old country, the land of his Italian extraction.

'Yeah, it feels good, I sleep better. I'm more at peace with myself. Pass the *burro*, please.'

'Here. What do you mean you're at war and peace with yourself?'

B hesitated for a moment. 'That's a good phrase.' I thought it

172

over and realized what I'd actually said. I had made up a good phrase.

B *burro*ed his toast. 'It's more like home in Italy. Monte Carlo was like Disneyland.'

We'd been in Monte Carlo for a little while before. We'd seen all the same people there that we'd seen in the winter in St Moritz and that we'd seen in the fall in Venice. I told B that they weren't just the 'international crowd' – they were like a whole new nationality. A nationality without a nation.

'Well, Europe is very mixed up now,' B said, 'since the War. There's a lot of intermarriage.'

'Fags with dykes?' I said that because it's one of B's favorite jokes. He was supposed to laugh, but he just let it pass.

'I mean French with Italian, Swiss with Greek. You know...'

'But B, why were there so many wars in Europe if the kings and queens all intermarried, because that means everybody was related, and why should people want to fight their relatives?' I ask that question a lot, because I always think about it – when I'm in Europe especially.

'Because nobody can fight more than relatives once they get started. Especially over some little prince. Like Princess Grace wants Princess Caroline to marry Prince Charles.'

I didn't get the point. B was just repeating an international fantasy rumor. Prince Charles would go backstage for Barbra Streisand as likely as he'd marry Princess Caroline. But you never know. 'Anyway,' B said, 'I'm not losing any sleep over it. Not in Italy.'

'But listen, B, about last night, if you're Italian yourself, why were you putting down the Prince – what's the cheese we had? The name of it?'

'Mozzarella.'

'Prince Mozzarella. Why did you put him down if he's Italian just like you. You should stick up for him.'

'I put him down because they said he was a hustler.'

He is a hustler. So what. We're hustlers, too.'

'And because he was fat.'

'All good hustlers are fat,' I reminded him.

'No, he shouldn't be fat. I would have liked him if he were a good-looking hustler.'

'Since when do you have to be good-looking to hustle? He made out a lot.'

B made a face. 'Right. He made a lot and spent it all on pasta.'

B was determined not to like Prince Mozzarella. I thought he was really funny, myself. But there was something else about dinner the night before that I wanted B to clear up for me:

'Who was that lady at my table?'

'Which lady? The one you were talking to all night? How can you be asking me who she was if you talked to her all through dinner? What did you talk about? She's the lady-in-waiting to Empress Soraya.'

'She's not Soraya's mother???' I couldn't believe it. That must have been why everyone was laughing. 'Are you sure, B?'

'Yes. She's Soraya's lady-in-waiting.'

'Then I made nothing but *faux pas* all through dinner . . .' I was trying to recall exactly what I'd said to her. I'd started off by complimenting her on having such a lovely daughter as Empress Soraya. She had so many jewels on I would never have thought she was a 'lady-in-waiting'. I didn't really have any concrete ideas about wl .. a lady-in-waiting should look like, but I always thought they were more like a maid. This lady had looked so rich.

'Ladies-in-waiting are all very high-class,' B explained. 'Some of them are even actual princesses. They *have* to be somebody important before they can "wait". Ladies have ladies-in-waiting so they – the ladies – don't have to go around alone.' This was starting to sound like *Guys And Dolls*.

'Is she a maid or not?' I asked B. That's what I wanted to know.

'No she's not a maid. She's someone who goes around with a person and does things for them, and waits for them while they do their things.'

'Well in that case,' I said, 'I'm a lady-in-waiting to my hairdresser.' My schedule depends on what he wants to do, I

174

have to go with him and wait around all day while he does business, and I can't leave until he leaves because I never know where I am or how to get back to where I've been, and if I did leave he'd yell at me when he found me.

B insisted that I was the 'Pope of Pop' and that a pope can't be a lady-in-waiting to a hairdresser. Theoretically, of course, that was true, but actually, I know when I'm a lady-in-waiting, no matter what they call it. It's one of my problems.

Everybody has problems, but the thing is to not make a problem about your Problem. For example, if you have no money and you worry about it all the time, you'll get an ulcer and have a real problem and you still won't have any money because people sense when you're desperate and nobody wants anything to do with a desperate person. But if you don't care about having no money, then people will give you money because you don't care and they'll think it's nothing and give it away – make you take it. But if you have a problem about having no money and taking money and think you can't take it and get guilty and want to be 'independent', then it's a problem. Whereas if you just take the money and act spoiled and spend it like it's nothing, then it's not a problem and people keep wanting to give you more.

The telephone rang.

B answered it. '*Pronto*.'

It was my art dealer in Torino, calling to invite us to lunch. I tried to motion to B that I wanted to go someplace where they'd have cherries.

When B got off the phone he said that we were meeting our dealer for lunch, and then he asked me, 'How do you get disciplined?'

'How does a person get disciplined?'

'Right. I want to know how you're supposed to pick up good habits. It's very easy to pick up bad ones. You always *want* to go after the bad habits. Say you eat ravioli one day and you like it so you eat it the next day and the next day and before you know it you have a ravioli habit or a pasta habit or a drug habit or a sex habit or a smoking habit or a cocaine habit . . .'

Was he trying to make me feel guilty about the cherries? 'You're asking me how you get out of the bad habits?' I asked him. No, he said he didn't want to know how you get out of the bad ones – just how you get into the good ones.

'Everybody has their good habits,' he said, 'that they do automatically that maybe they learned when they were little – brushing your teeth, not talking with your mouth full, saying excuse me – but other good habits – like writing a chapter a day or jogging every morning – are harder to get into. That's what I mean by "discipline" – how do you get new, good habits? I'm asking you because you're so disciplined.'

'No, I'm not disciplined, really,' I said. 'It just looks that way because I do what people tell me to do and I don't complain about it while it's happening.' That's a three-part rule of mine: (1) never complain about a situation while the situation is still going on; (2) if you can't believe it's happening, pretend it's a movie; and (3) after it's over, find somebody to pin the blame on and never let them forget it. If the person you pin the blame on is smart they'll turn it into a running joke so whenever you bring it up you can both laugh about it, and that way the horrible situation can turn out to be fun in retrospect. (But it all depends on how mercilessly you hound the person you're blaming, because they'll only make a joke out of it when they're desperate, and the more desperate you make them by hounding them, the better the joke they'll make out of it.)

'It's not discipline, B,' I repeated. 'It's knowing what you really want.' Anything a person really wants is okay with me.

'All right. But let's take champagne. All my life I wanted as much champagne as I could drink, but now that I'm getting all the champagne I ever wanted and more, look what I'm getting – a double chin!'

'You're also finding out that champagne isn't what you really want, since you don't want a double chin. You're finding out that champagne isn't what you want, it's beer you want.'

'Then I'd get a beer belly.' B laughed at the idea of a champagne chin and a beer belly.

'Then beer isn't what you want, either.'

'But that's not hard to figure out – nobody wants beer.'

'Yes they do,' I told him. 'You're the one who told the joke about an Irish seven-course dinner being a boiled potato and a six-pack.'

'Yes, I suppose . . . But it's not the thing I want so much as the idea of the thing.'

'Then that's just advertising,' I reminded him.

'Right, but it works because the reason I want champagne, the reason most people want champagne, is they're impressed with the idea – Champagne! – like they're impressed with the idea of caviar. Champagne and caviar is status.'

That was not completely true. In some society shit is status. 'Look,' I told him, 'you realized when you ended up with a double chin that your values were misplaced. Right? It takes time to find out, but you're finding out. Even today you put your nose up in the air if you don't have dinner with the Afghanellis, the Cuchinellis, the Pickinellis, the Mountbottoms, the Van Tissens—'

B cut me off, screaming, 'I do not! I'd rather have dinner every night with the kids at the office!'

'Oh sure,' I said. Who was he trying to kid? 'Listen, I know you. You can't wait to get back to town and tell everybody a million times that you had dinner with the Dukarnos.'

'So will you! So will you! You'll act bored about it when you tell it and I'll act excited about it when I tell it and that's the only difference! I'm telling you, I'd rather have dinner with cute kids my own age!'

'When are you going to start entertaining at home, B? You haven't had one party at your house. You live in the right neighborhood, the Upper East Side, so what are you waiting for?'

'It's too small. It's just a studio.'

'You live in a studio?? You didn't tell me. How great.' I want to live in a studio. In one room. That's what I've always wanted, not have anything – to be able to get rid of all my junk – maybe put everything on microfilm or holographic wafers – and just move into one room. I was really jealous of B's lifestyle.

'Are you air-conditioned?' I asked, jealously.

'Yes.'

'Built-in?'

'Yes. You're always so impressed with air conditioning. Maybe I should give a party. I'll wait for a heat wave and the air conditioning can be the theme of the party. But my studio is too small to stay in more than an hour and a half, because after an hour people start to get claustrophobic. The best kind of party I could give would be champagne and nuts and then take everybody dancing.'

It was time to start getting ready for lunch. B went back to his room to dress. I put my napkin over the bowl of cherry pits so I wouldn't have to look at how many I'd eaten. That's the hard part of overdosing on cherries – you have all the pits to tell you exactly how many you ate. Not more or less. Exactly. One-seed fruits really bother me for that reason. That's why I'd always rather eat raisins than prunes. Prune pits are even more imposing than cherry pits.

14 The Tingle

In New York I spend most of my morning talking on the phone to one B or another. I call it 'checking-in'. I like to hear about everything the B did since the morning before. I ask about all the places I didn't go and all the people I didn't see. Even if a B accompanied me to a party or a club the night before I ask what happened because I may have missed something on the other side of the room. If I didn't miss it, I forgot it.

I have no memory. Every day is a new day because I don't remember the day before. Every minute is like the first minute of my life. I try to remember but I can't. That's why I got married – to my tape recorder. That's why I seek out people with minds like tape recorders to be with. My mind is like a tape recorder with one button – Erase.

If I wake up too early to check in with anyone, I kill time by watching TV and washing my underwear. Maybe the reason my memory is so bad is that I always do at least two things at once. It's easier to forget something you only half-did or quarter-did.

My favorite simultaneous action is talking while eating. I think it's a sign of class. The rich have many advantages over the poor, but the most important one, as far as I'm concerned, is knowing how to talk and eat at the same time. I think they learn it in finishing school. It's very important if you go out to dinner a lot. At dinner you're expected to eat – because if you don't it's an insult to the hostess – and you're expected to talk – because if you don't it's an insult to the other guests. The rich somehow manage to work it out but I just can't do it. They are never caught with an open mouth full of food but that's what happens to me. It's always my turn to talk just when I've filled my mouth with mashed potatoes. The rich, on the other hand, seem to take turns automatically; one talks while the other chews; then one chews while the other talks. If for some reason the conversation demands an immediate comment in the middle of chewing, the rich know how to quickly hide the half-chewed food somewhere – under the tongue? behind the teeth? halfway down the throat? – while they make their point. When I ask my rich friends how they do it, they say, 'Do what?' That's how much they take it for granted. I practice at home in front of the mirror and over the phone. In the meantime, until I've perfected the ability to talk and eat simultaneously, I stick to my basic rule for dinner party behavior: don't talk and don't eat.

Of course you can have bad manners if you know how to use them.

One morning I was vacuuming while watching Capital Punishment on Barbara Walters and the phone rang. I knew it was a particular B because she's the only one who calls me before I call her. All the other Bs wait for me to make the first move. This B is a conceptual thinker from a good family. Though she has moved to the wrong side of the tracks her breeding still shows. She can eat, talk, and *walk* at the same time.

I let the phone ring ten times because Capital Punishment was riveting. Finally I picked it up and said quickly, 'Hi, could you hold on for a second.' I dropped the receiver and ran into the kitchen for some toast with jam. While I waited for the toast to toast I read the label on the jar of jam. I took the jar back with me to the phone because I like to spoon it out onto the toast, glob by glob, bite by bite.

'What's new,' I said, pressing my ear to the receiver, my mouth to the jam.

B gave me a blow-by-blow description of the Barbara Walters show. I wasn't bored because I had forgotten it already. When she got to the point where she was describing what I was watching on my TV in front of me, I interrupted.

'What else is new?'

'I don't know,' snapped B, who hates to be interrupted. 'What are you doing?'

'Cleaning up.'

'Cleaning is a thing that bugs me twenty-four hours a day,' B answered. She's the kind of person who always has the same problem as you do, only a million times more. 'I always have it on my mind,' she continued enthusiastically. 'Where to clean next – a drawer? the desk? the closet? I've vacuumed the room but I haven't vacuumed the closet, and I'm really going to get it all done today. I've got to shampoo the rug first. I've been using Old Glory Extra-Professional-Strength shampoo and I do it just the way they say – by putting a six-inch-by-six-inch patch. Then I scrub it with a brush and bring the nap up, then I leave the room with a lot of stuff for about three hours – a tape recorder, a couple of books, magazines, newspapers – and I go to the park and sit there and talk to the bums. Then I can come back and vacuum up all the foam. I have to make sure I have new E-11 bags because I have a Singer vacuum cleaner, the canister type. I wish I had a Hoover. Most people don't use their vacuum cleaners because they have to put them in the mop closets and if you're at somebody's house and ask to use their vacuum cleaner they say, "Oh, don't bother, it's so heavy, it's such a mess," and so they use carpet sweepers. And carpet sweepers are really out of date. Carpet sweepers and a broom. You don't bring up the nap on a rug with a broom. Because all you do then is get little broom hairs all over the rug, and then you have to pick those up individually and put them in the waste-paper basket, and then you've got more garbage. Unless you put them down the toilet. So then I start vacuuming. I have to decide what I'm going to do first. The floor? No. Because the dirt darts in other places. So if I haven't made my bed yet I vacuum along the bottom of the bed. With no extra equipment on the end of the thing. I just put maybe the long tube with the very tight plastic thing with just a little hole. So I can get into the corners. Then I have to do my desk. I take all the books off. I put the brush attachment on – the round brush – take my telephone book, go along the top of it with the brush and then all down the edges. If I see a spot on my alligator pocketbook which is maybe on the desk next to the phone book I have to get my shoe-shine bag out of the closet and get my saddle soap and clean that. I clean everything so

183

meticulously there's nothing messy or dirty in the room. In the house. Nothing. NOTHING!'

'Don't shout, B,' I said, spooning out a little more jam.

'Okay, but say my pocket radio's next to the telephone book. Well, after I've dusted that with the vacuum cleaner I take it out of its little leather case and vacuum the inside of that, and while I'm doing that I open the radio up and put in a new nine-volt battery and then, using the attachment with the little hole, I vacuum the inside of the radio because it keeps the battery thing free of dust and you don't get static on your radio. Then there's the jar of pencils on my desk. I take all the pencils out of the jar and put them on newspaper but I have to put the newspaper on the bathroom floor because I don't want the print to rub off on the rug or bedspread. Then I put the little pencil jar in hot Ivory soap and a little Fantastik and I started about a month ago using those – not Brillo pads, they have no soap in them – you know, they're like those wire things that might make an Art Deco pin or something? Those little wire soap pads that get the stuck ink and pencil shavings out of the bottom of the jar. Then, before I put the pencils all back, I have to make sure they're sharpened finely so I get the pencil sharpener out of the top drawer of my desk and I go back in the bathroom and sharpen my pencils over the toilet, because if I do it in my room over the waste basket, some of the dust is going to back up into the air, and it'll probably settle somewhere I've already cleaned, and I really want to GET FREE OF ALL THE DUST. After sharpening my pencils I flush the shavings and put the pencils back in the little jar. Then I take all the books off the shelves and put them in the bathroom on top of the newspaper. Then I you know, once-over it with the brush. Vacuum. Then I have to shine it. I get the Endust out. It's better than Old Gold or Pledge or Lemon Pledge. That's such a farce, adding all those lemons to everything. Lemon was 1973. I think. Everything was coming up lemons. This year everything's a "tingle". So the Endust does that tingle to the furniture. I spray it on a clean yellow cloth. I have to remember, after I've done all my dusting, to wash the

184

cloth. I just go over the shelves with it. I have a little thing with my cigarettes in it – not a box, sort of a glass – and I take all the cigarettes out and shake that into the toilet so I won't have little pieces of tobacco lying around. Then I go through the next little tin that has only pens in it, and scissors and Exacto knives and things like that, and I check to make sure all the ballpoint pens are writing. If they don't write on the first letter, I throw them right out in the garbage can. I've got a nice garbage liner twenty-two by forty-four in the garbage can so I don't have to wash the pail after I finish throwing everything out. Then I take the brush attachment and brush all the books. Down the sides, on the top. If the covers look sloppy or ragged, I take a little bit of ConTact paper covering just the outside part of the book and I type up a label in a matching color and put it down the spine of the book. If I have an old book, like say, Sherlock Holmes, that has a raggedy-edged cover, well, I take the cover off, and then, if it isn't a pretty-color book that matches the room – say it's dark brown and I don't like dark brown, I like yellow – I use ConTact paper. That way I have some continuity on my bookshelves. After that I have to vacuum the typewriter. That's such a drag. I've got to be careful or I can ruin my machine. I've got the vacuum out and I leave on the same brush attachment. I turn it on and I just brush lightly through the keys. Then I put on the long narrow hose and I unscrew the top part of the typewriter with a screwdriver and then I work on each key. I get a bottle of denatured alcohol, and a whole box of Q-tips. I plan on wasting them. Because I can only use one side for each letter. And since there's two letters on each key I have to use one Q-tip for each key. Then I blow a little bit with my mouth onto the typewriter to get the dust going toward the big hole. Then I vacuum it up. Then I get the Fantastik out and I put it on one of those reusable – Handi-Wipes, they call them. They come in yellow and white, and turquoise and white, and pink and white. I use yellow and white. Everything this year is green and white and yellow and white. Not lemon, just yellow, I don't know why. I put a little of the Fantastik on the Handi-Wipe and

I go between each key with a Q-tip and a little Fantastik just to be sure the white parts between the black keys are clean. Anybody with a piano should do the same. You have to be careful not to let any of the Fantastik drip into where the keys are because that's going to ruin the insides of the typewriter. Then I have to make sure all the plugs are clean. I have to see if they're unplugged so I don't get a shock. White extension cords get dirty. When I have one that looks too dirty I take it off and make a list on a little white pad – "new extension cord, 6 inches". Then I start doing the drawers of the desk. I have a lot of tapes in the top drawer so I have to see that all the cassettes are in order. I take a whole line of them out and put them on newspaper. Then I spray Fantastik down that space and with my Handi-Wipes I wipe that up. And then I take each cassette and I dust and wipe each one with a tiny bit of Windex which is good for their plastic coverings. I never get them out of line or out of order, they stay right in line because once I mixed up two years and it took me a long time to put it back together line by line, date by date. And then I usually get a little distracted because I see a tape and think, "Oh, gosh, that person's dead, and I should listen to it for a minute." So I just quickly get that done. And then I go to the second drawer which is filled with stationery: yellow legal pads on the bottom, smaller legal pads on top, then a little smaller, and envelopes in the cross-way – everything is a perfect fit. So I take out everything and check through and see if I still want it. Like, I have two pads that are from an art-supply store that are to write up television commercials and they have a shape of a television on them. Well, I know I'll probably never use them. Then I go through the envelopes. I've neatly labeled with the typewriter what's in the envelope. If the label gets dirty and raggedy-looking I type a new one. If it's for letters I'm saving, I go through the letters to see if I still want to save them. Well, I might find a few birthday cards. You know, from people who were sentimental to me a year ago. I toss them right out. And also if they're not particularly pretty – out. I don't want to bother to file them with "Famous

People's Cards". I have postcards that are the large size that should go in a postcard-collecting box but I've forgotten to buy the postcard-collecting box so I write that down to buy. I measure the postcards first. And I go to Goldsmith Brothers and buy the box when I have enough money. Then there's all my little address books. I've got Europe, England, Spain, Rome, Paris, all with a rubber band around them. And then I've got diaries from Paris and last year's calendar which is always good to keep for taxes, and little trip books from the 60s that I really don't need but I really don't want to get rid of because they might be worth something later. When they revive the 60s. I take them all out and I get the vacuum cleaner with the brush part attached and then I pick up the extra dust there and take the ConTact paper out – there's ConTact paper at the bottom of my drawers – because I want to dust under the ConTact paper. I want to get to the wood—'

'Hello?' As usual we were cut off. B lives in a small residential hotel with an overworked switchboard. Every now and then the switchboard operator pulls the plug out on B because she feels B has had more than her fair share of talking time. Then B has to wait a few minutes for a new line. She doesn't really mind and neither do I – it gives us both a chance to go to the bathroom or something. This time, however, it was twenty minutes before B called me back. I really don't need that much time in the bathroom. I was tempted to call up another B to kill time but just as I was about to dial, the phone rang and this B was back.

'Sorry, bad board today,' she said.

'But I was waiting twenty minutes.'

'A, I'm not thinking about time, I'm thinking about DETAIL!' she roared. 'I'm thinking about all the cleaning I have to do! After I finish the stationery drawer, after I vacuum all the little plain white pads and the airmail envelopes, take them all out, put them back in, I still have to do the bottom drawer, the drawer filled with pictures. There are a lot of envelopes that say "Miscellaneous" in that drawer and this is one of the things I'm trying to conquer in my life, the word "Miscellaneous". It's got to go. Because nothing is miscellaneous. So I've decided to take everything that's in "Miscellaneous" and put it in another file. So I take out things like "Releases", and envelopes people have sent me with a picture I sent to somebody who died, and photographs from books, all these things. And I say, "Do I really want all these releases?" So I open the packages and I look. Well, I won't have all the releases, I'll just save the important ones. The rest I'll throw out. I'll get rid of a good eighth of an inch if I throw out somebody like – Lee Tallberg. Who the hell is Lee Tallberg? Rotten Rita? Well, maybe Rotten Rita I should keep. Peter Hugall . . . well, maybe I'll save releases. Maybe I'll make a book of releases. I'll keep them in the same envelope and just have it published like it is. "Releases in an Envelope." Then I have to go through the Guarantee File. Now, there's no point in keeping guarantees that are over the ninety-day guarantee period. So I go through the envelope and I get rid of a good inch when I throw out guarantees from 1965, you know, tape recorders and cameras, and I've mailed in the warranty and I save the little thing but they send me after a year an IBM card that says, "If you require service on any of these parts you pay $17.00." Then, of course, I have my receipts for taxes for three years and each month – I keep them very neat, they're in business envelopes – they don't fit very well, but I keep all of 1973 in a manila file that says "Receipts". Then Xeroxes of things I keep because there was a reason for me to Xerox them in the first place, so there's no reason for me to go through them. Then "Ideas". Well, the idea envelope is empty, but I might get some so I might as well keep the envelope for the file. "Bills to Be Paid." Well, actually, "Bills to Be Paid" isn't a good file to keep hidden in a drawer, so if I want to be a better housekeeper I should actually take those bills out that I might have to pay and keep them in sight. "Lawyer." Well, all the letters from the lawyer are dated and I keep them in order with the last letter that he sent me at the top. That file I'll keep. "Letters to Write." Now that's another stupid file because there's only one letter in it, to Heiner Friedrich and John Giorno to send back

something and I know I'll never mail it, so I'm going to throw it
out and that's about an eighth of an inch gone now. Now,
"Carbon Copies of Letters." That's a good file because they were
funny letters that I wrote. "Possibilities for Movies." That's a
good file too. I haven't thought of any yet but I'm always
thinking. Now my "Accountant" envelope I'm keeping. That I
even add to, every time I see an article like in *New York* magazine
about deducting your plants. I cut it out and put it in the file for
the accountant – "Powers of Deduction" – writing off the home
office – so I'll know for next year. "The Dope Lawyer." That's a
script. Well, there's no reason not to save scripts. "School
Play." That's an original screenplay written in hand. Now, I've
got a little thing of foreign coins here. I guess the only ones I
should bother to save are kopeks because there's not enough
English money here, it's all Russian money, so I'll keep it. So that
drawer's neat. Now I have to get my Handi-Wipe and dust the
desk with Endust and go all around the edges. Then I have to get
the most horrible product there is out of the waste-paper basket
I keep under the sink in the bathroom. It's Noxon. It really is
the smelliest product made. But I have to do the hardware on the
desk. The little handles. I tear a pillowcase up because a rag isn't
right. I've got to really get into all the edges with the Noxon.
There are six fixtures on the desk and I might as well do the
doorknobs too. Once it gets dry I put the Noxon on and then I
polish it with another cleaning rag, so it's all shiny. Then for a
week or so if I want it to stay nice and gold like that, I put on
those white sleeping gloves every time I open my desk. Then I
realize that I have my bureau drawer to do. Then I realize that
I forgot that silver glass I keep pencils in. I might as well polish
all the silver at the same time. So I go and take out my one silver
spoon – stolen from my mother's – and a little silver demitasse
spoon for when I'm in the mood, and my silver glass, and my
silver key chain, and I go in the bathroom and get out my Gorham
Silver Polish, and I put on my lined yellow rubber gloves. Lined
so they don't stick to my fingers. But first I powder my hands
with Johnson's Baby Powder – silver polish, and Noxon too, is

very hard on your hands, they make them dry. A very funny feeling, like when you get a dry mouth. Then I clean the silver with a little cloth, then I rinse it in warm soapy water, then I polish it. But since I don't want to dirty another cloth I usually polish it with toilet paper. Then there's a flower vase on the desk I want to clean, so I put it in soapy water, and then I stick toilet paper down into the center to dry the base. Then, after that I have to do the top drawer.'

'You already did the top drawer,' I noted through the jam.

'That was the top drawer of my desk,' B growled. 'I still have to do the top drawer of my bureau. And then I have to start vacuuming because if I'd done the vacuuming first I'd have all the dust back again. So anyway, I do the top drawer. I pull it out. No matter how many times I clean it, it's always a mess. I can keep it clean for exactly one hour after I've cleaned it. I have to accept in my mind that this is a never-ending thing. The top drawer is always going to be messy and I'm always going to have to vacuum. I mean, if I order coffee in the morning and I'm pouring sugar from the little bag into the cup, well, some of those little granules are going to fall on top of the bureau, or on the floor. I may not feel that little granule of sugar but I know it's there. I may not see it, but I know there's dirt there. Then there's a part of the rug, that's sort of worn, you know, where there's a line and you can see just the thread maybe and no color. I go through all my Magic Markers till I find the right color. I test it on a piece of white paper, then I very lightly try to cover the gray line that has no carpet on it so it matches the rug. Now, my eyeglasses look filthy in here. I take them out of the drawer and put them on another piece of newspaper. On top of the towel on the bed. I don't dare put them on top of the bedspread that I brought back from the cleaners yesterday. Then, let's see. Eyedrops. Well, there's five bottles of eyedrops here: there's Collyrium, there's Visine, there's Murine Number Two, there's French Couleur Bleu – now *they're* not dirty but all their little caps are. They all need a once-over with Fantastik. And a dusting. So they get put on top of the towel too. Now there's a jar of Vaseline Intensive

Care cream. Now *it's* not dirty but the top has coffee grains on it, a few crystals of salt, a hair, some lint . . . if I look at it closely with a magnifying glass maybe I'll see that some soup dropped on it. So that needs to be cleaned with Fantastik. I take everything out of the top drawer and put it on top of the towel. Then I take the vacuum cleaner with the brush part and I brush and vacuum every empty space and partition. Then I go to the bathroom and make sure that the sink is really clean. I take some Lysol Basin Cleaner. Not Lysol spray for bad odors, not Lysol for john-bowls. This is Lysol for basins and tubs. And it's a spray. I spray the basin and the inside hole and down the drain-hole. I've got my rubber gloves on. Then I wash my brushes and combs to get them sterile. Then I put my five combs and my Mason Pearson hairbrush – but first I look in my jacket to make sure I don't have any combs in there and in the closet too – and then I put them in some Ivory Liquid Detergent. I let them all soak for five or ten minutes and after that I take a handbrush or nailbrush – the kind I like are from the hardware store, they cost thirty-five or thirty-seven cents and you can buy them now with white bristles which I think look nicer in the bathroom than the natural bristles. It looks nice and clean with white bristles. Then with each comb I go back and forth twice, once on each side with the handbrush in soapy water. Then I run the soapy water out of the sink and I go to the bathtub and hold each comb under the running water to rinse it. Then I lay all the combs and the brush on top of a white handtowel and wrap them up. And then I lay them on the windowsill for fifteen minutes to dry, but I leave them wrapped so they won't get dirty from the soot. So those are clean. Then I have a plastic box where I keep all my nail things, my tweezers, my pimple squeezers – now the thing I remember while I'm cleaning is I'm not just trying to clean everything to put it back where it was – I'm trying to ELIMINATE too. So if I have ten pairs of tweezers in there why not get the mirror out quickly and tweezer a few hairs here and there to be sure the tweezer works. Once I've done that I look on the tweezers to make sure there's no caked honey on it or anything like that. If it looks clean and it works, I put it back in its little tweezer holder. If the tweezer is no good, I take an envelope out of my desk – a white envelope – and put it into my typewriter and type, "Tweezer to Be Repaired." Then I take the clippers – they're usually in good condition because I usually put them in their clipper cases. They look dirty and dusty because the clipper cases are clear plastic on top. But they're not dirty on the outside because all the clippers have been kept inside a plastic box inside the bureau, but what looks dirty and dull is the inside of the plastic. So I have to take a piece of cloth and cut it – with a little Fantastik on it, and just stuff it down inside the case so the plastic gets clear-looking like glass. You know? Then I can put my little clippers back in. And I pour everything else out, like nail-whitener, and, oh, a few things like those wooden sticks for my nails. Well, if I see any that are dirty or that the points aren't sharp – I toss them right out into the waste basket and put it on another list. Insert it in the typewriter and put, "Things to Buy". Underline it and put "Orange Sticks". That's what they're called. Then I go through the eyebrow pencils and . . .'

Just then I yawned. Unfortunately I was spooning some more jam into my mouth and because of the yawn it got sucked in too far and my throat rejected it and spat it out all over the receiver. I dropped everything and ran to the kitchen for a paper towel and came back and wiped the receiver off. Hearing all this on her end of the line, B assumed that I was bored with our conversation, but I wasn't. I just got caught eating and talking – yawning is a way of talking – at the same time.

'. . . okay, okay, okay, so I've got the whole top thing cleaned, I've emptied it and I've cleaned it. Now, I take my Hoover, the most old-fashioned kind, the best kind, the dirty old Hoover. But it's so hard to maneuver. I prefer the canister type. I have to do the venetian blinds. Those I can always see the dust on and it drives me crazy! Crazy. Because I can really see it. And if I touch it with my fingers, I know it's blowing in the air. So I get up on a chair with the vacuum cleaner in my left hand, I've got the brush part on again and I'm – oh, I take the venetian blind and pull the string so they're open, kind of, and I go along back and forth. Then – I've vacuumed all the dust off – I've got to wash the blinds. So here I am stark raving naked at the window and I want to wash my blinds. I'm so hot from cleaning and vacuuming – you see, people don't understand that vacuums are like toys. You know, like when children are given a five-and-ten-cent cart of little robots that they can turn on and make walk around a room. I mean that they could actually decorate like a toy. A canister vacuum cleaner could look like a little horse, it would look cute in a child's room just sitting there. I hang mine on the back of the bathroom door. And I keep all my attachments there. So once I've gotten all the dust off the blinds, because if I wash them with all the dust on, I've got a bathtub full of dust. Then I take the blinds down and I take one whole bottle of Zud – a can of Zud – and I mix it with aluminum ammonia. It really stinks. Then I put my blinds in the bathtub. I always wear my rubber gloves for this. Then I vacuum all the other drawers and the floor. What I basically want to do is raise the nap of the rug but before I start to vacuum I pick up every little thing I can find on the rug. If I see a spot, I get out my shampoo. There's a new kind of shampoo now that's supposed to be just spray and vacuum. So I spray, and it penetrates into the nap and in a few minutes I vacuum it up and it's clean. For the spots on the rugs I use those little spot-sticks. Renuzit, cleaning fluid – anything like that. I use that very small attachment. Because I get down on my knees when I vacuum and I always do it nude – I never vacuum with my clothes on – and I go back and forth in a vertical motion, very quickly with the little tiny attachment. And I look closely to make sure I've picked up everything and I think, "Oh, God, why am I getting all those yellow bathroom-rug fibers when it's a turquoise rug?" What I'm picking up is actually yellow! Because it's all stuck, you see, to the edge of the vacuum cleaner part. So I do it as well as I can, I go to all the corners, and then when I get to a corner of the rug I even pick it up. So I decide, "I'm going to, just for the excitement of it, run it along quickly underneath." Underneath, below the tag, where the floor is getting old and cracked and there's a few nails. I can always hear "ZZZZDDDZZZZZPPPP" and I'm picking up a lot. When I get to the closet I get really excited, I take everything out and I've always got five hundred million pieces of chipped paint that have fallen from the walls of the closet onto the floor, and I can hear those go click up the vacuum cleaner, and I love it. I really love the feeling of hearing it go up. I guess as much as I love to vacuum-clean ashtrays – you see, if it were like a child's toy, always parked and plugged in, like a bicycle, it would be so great to just – zip right through the house. But it's the big hang-up of taking it out of closets, being heavy, other people complaining. When I was a kid and I had to clean up after a party, I was the first one who ever thought of putting forty extension cords on a vacuum cleaner and going out by the pool to pick up forty million thousand peanut shells from the grass. Nobody else had ever thought of that. The dumb caretakers were too dumb. They'd just say, "Go out and pick them up." Well there I was picking them up with my fingers, but did I ever shock them when they were going back and forth on their lawn mowers and I was out there maneuvering my Hoover on the grass. That way it took me only five minutes to pick up the peanut shells.

'And then there's loose tea from teabags inside the box where I have the teabags. Lipton's tea. There's like, forty-five packages. Well, I take all the teabags out of the box and vacuum the bottom, because some of the tea has come out of the bags . . . and then, I get petrified that my neighbors are going to hear this vacuum cleaner going all the time and I keep wondering do they think they're listening to a room that has maid service at two in the morning and is preparing for a new guest? You know? I keep on forgetting I still have to vacuum all my shopping bags because they all have residue on the bottom. You know, there might be an odd little piece of paper at the bottom of the bags, a peanut, a granola, anything. I have to put the bag right on the floor and I have to put my two feet into it. Then I can put the hose to it. Otherwise, I mean if you hold the shopping bag and vacuum it that way, you vacuum up the bag. Then I vacuum-clean my plants.

194

I have to be very delicate. I only vacuum-clean the dirt part, the bottom of the dish where the water's supposed to drain to. And very very lightly I vacuum-clean the dust off the leaves. Then I open up the air conditioner where the screen is and I turn off the air conditioner and I vacuum the screen inside the filter and then vacuum around the bottom of it and along the top and underneath and around the windowsill and if everything doesn't come off, if everything isn't right, I write on my pad of "Things to Do" to paint the spot on the windowsill, to paint the part of the radiator that's turning brown.

'I might paint the vacuum too – green or yellow for the summer – and find a place for it. They're just so great. On the bottom, you can take the hose part with the suction, and screw it onto the bottom of the vacuum cleaner, and get blow-out air. One day I didn't have my hairdryer and I thought I could use that to dry my hair. So I attached the hose to the blow-out part and I blew out everything that was in the bag. It blew all over into little pieces of dust. One thing, you can always tell when your habits change by checking that bag.

'And A, you know how I care what the outside of my door looks like. I can hear the maid doing the hallway – she doesn't do it with a vacuum, she does it with a broom, and she vacuums the dust out of the room across the way with a broom too. Well, it's my territory and I feel that it's wrong of her to do that. So I have to vacuum up the hall. And one day, belligerently, because they don't wash the walls outside my room, I was out there with my African dress on and I was washing a wall, because I was testing a new product on their wall before I used it on my own. I was using Big Wally. I get all these products from television. So I was out using Big Wally on the walls and I was doing it and the maid kept looking at me, she wasn't saying anything. But I was giving the hint to her, like – "I know, the union doesn't let you do that." '

For some reason, this conversation was making me very hungry. But I was getting tired of plain grape jam. I wanted something more exotic, like guava. So I very gently put down the receiver and tip-toed into the kitchen. B talked on.

'That reminds me of art in the toilet. It started this way. One day I decided to tear up all the nude pictures of myself. I was vacuuming my Polaroids – I had just finished up vacuuming my checkbooks – and I decided that I had to vacuum all the little boxes where I keep my Polaroids because they were filled with food and hairs. I don't know if it happens to everyone, I don't know how I always get the stray hair in the drawer when I open it, I just can't figure it out. Anyway, I have to take all the Polaroids and like I did with the tapes I have to keep them all in order because they're all in files. So, this one day, I decided to go through the pictures of myself, all my self-photographs where I would kneel down, pull in my cheeks, put my tits together, and take pictures of myself. So I went through the file and the ones that weren't any good I tore up and put in the waste basket. And the next day the engineer came up here and he said – I'd called him to borrow another five dollars or something, because money is another thing like cleaning that I worry about terribly – but anyway, I asked him if I could borrow another five, and he said, yes, he's a Negro engineer, and then, he said, "I have something very close to you right here." and he patted his left-hand shirt pocket. And I said, "What's that, John?" And he said, "I've got it very close to me, right here," and he took it out, and he had pasted it back together and there it was. A nude picture of me. Well, with that, I started to be really selective about what I sent down to the end of the hall. A lot of times now I take things in shopping bags out of the hotel and put them in the garbage can a block down on the corner. I have to go through the whole thing, because sometimes when I start to flush it down the toilet, I don't want the people across the hall to think that I have diarrhea for three hours while I'm flushing. Like *TV Guide*. Or an empty cigarette pack. I don't want to put them in the waste-paper basket because I want that EMPTY so I sit on the edge of the bath-tub and I take two pages of *TV Guide* at a time and I tear it up into four or five pieces, put it in the toilet, flush, and I go through that with the whole *TV Guide*. You know, if I've come back from emptying the trash and I see, "Oh, that's last

196

Saturday's *Guide*." Then I do it with an empty box of cigarettes. I take the silver paper out and I crumple that in a ball – I put that in the toilet – then I take the little box of Marlboros and make it into little pieces. I decided I can get pretty much down the toilet. Oh, then I remember that I've had milk sitting on the windowsill for four hours, and I think it's going bad, but I never taste it to see if it is, so I pour the milk in, and then I have to come in for the scissors because I can't rip the carton sometimes because of the arthritis in my left fingers so I have to cut the milk carton up into squares and flush that and that's about four flushes . . . HELLO . . . HELLO . . .'

'Hello,' I said, returning just in time with some apple butter and a fresh spoon.

'I hate it when you leave me, A. If I could talk to myself I would, but I can't. That's why I need you.' B was on the verge of tears. She is very sentimental about our conversations.

'Okay, I'm listening,' I told her, unscrewing the brand new jar of apple butter.

'Sometimes I flush tons of food out. Like yesterday, I'll tell you what I threw away in the toilet. Do you want to hear?'

'What are you waiting for?'

'Okay, okay. I flushed down six times the heads of radishes, two plastic bags, one was a carrot bag, one was the radish bag, and one paper bag that the carrots and radishes had come in from the store. And then I flushed down the tops of the carrots and the bottoms of the carrots. Then I tore up the paper plate where I put the Krazy Mixed-up salt that I dipped the carrots and radishes into, and I tore up the paper plate and put that into the toilet. I flush each thing separately so that's fifteen flushes right there. Then, old pills I flush, too. And then, when I get very nervous when I hear the commercial on the radio. "This is the one number you must know thump thump thump thump thump. Do you know your number? Have your blood pressure taken!" At that point I think I'm going to die so then I think, "Oh, God! better throw some of the pornography away." So, back to the drawer of the Polaroids. Yesterday I decided to throw out the

197

nude boys. I took the file card that says "Cocks, Young", and I tore it up to pieces and I flushed it, then I flushed the boys down. Then when I had muscle magazines to do the cock collages, people would give me the magazines, I was very paranoid that I was going to get busted with these magazines. So I cut all the cocks out and put them in a tiny little brown envelope, but then I had the magazines to contend with . I was too paranoid to leave them at the end of the hall so I had to cut each magazine into little squares and flush the muscle magazines down. Then I've got a lot of things that they say can't be flushed. I had a problem once when I flushed a dropcloth. That was when I had covered the rug with a plastic dropcloth because I was having a boy paint the room, and after he was done I cleaned up the room, emptied everything, but I'd forgotten the dropcloth. So I cut it into four squares and I started to flush the dropcloth, and it became a bubble and it came out of the toilet. So. Art in the Toilet and Art in the Bathtub. A friend of mine told me that his psychiatrist had recommended as therapy that he fingerpaint while he was in the shower. So I really saw the fingerpaints in his apartment but not in the shower. Because if you fingerpaint in the shower on the tiles, it just washes away while you're taking the shower, it's clean when you come out. So I decided to paint – when I stopped doing all that arty stuff and stopped buying Dr Martin's watercolors, dyes and Magic Markers and all that stuff, because it made such a mess – I mean, I had to have a little glass of water, I had to have a little plastic thing to keep my brushes clean, I had to then clean my paint sets with something else, which was really a work in the toilet – to run water over a whole box of watercolors so that each color would stay its own color, because I'd get orange and green and black all in one little pellet, so I'd use up half a box letting hot water run into the watercolors and then try to blot it out with toilet paper and flush it down the toilet to clean the paintbox. So I said, "No more painting, NO MORE ART!" Then I said, "I've got to use up all these supplies, all the Dr Martin's watercolor dyes so I can throw them out." I would have thrown them out full but I said, "To hell with it, I'll

make a movie. I'll throw them out in the tub." So I took pink
and I just squirted pink down the bathtub. Then I took a little bit
of turquoise blue and I squirted that next to the pink with a
white towel in between and then I added a little water to it and
got this beautiful pattern, and I put a sunlamp on top where the
shower curtain is and it was beautiful, and I started to film it with
a Super-eight movie camera and I emptied the bottle of dyes and
they were in the plastic liners in the trash can, and then I just
turned on the water faucets and I had a clean surface and I hadn't
made a bit of a mess and yet I had a whole painting. I Polaroided it
and I still have the Polaroid. Then I decided I could do Roy
Lichtenstein in the toilet so easily. I wanted to get rid of all those
little round balls that I have from the sixties Psychedelic Art
sticker period, so I went through a drawer and as I went through
I thought to throw all the dots from Childcraft, throwing all the
dots in the clean white toilet and they were floating around and
looking so pretty because the bowl was clean, I'd put Comet in
before, green Comet – and used a johnny brush, so it was really
white – and I took a Polaroid of the dots and it looked just like
a Lichtenstein, and then I flushed the dots and the painting was
gone. And then I had some little American flags – I don't know, I
read on the street that you get arrested if you put an American
flag on an envelope and so I thought I'd do some Jasper Johns on
the toilet. I threw all my American flags into the toilet and then I
had a Polaroid Jasper Johns. I did a Warhol in the john too, using
the Dr Scholl's liners from the insides of my shoe. They were
really ratty and they were sticking to my feet, so I thought I might
as well get rid of them. So I put them in the toilet and took the
Polaroid and they looked like the dance-step painting. Flushed
those down. It was hard for me to do a Rauschenberg so I just
threw an announcement for his show down. I flushed it and it
stayed up so I had to cut it. It's the same thing with the laundry.
In a way, watching something flush is like watching the spin cycle
in a laundry-mat. Or drying in a dryer. You get incredible
patterns. When something's on a spin cycle, even if it's a print – all
prints of tulips and everything – it looks like a Kenneth Noland

in the dryer. It has all straight lines. Just on the spin cycle. Or in the dryer when it's going really fast. Or on the extractor cycle. I buy Marlboro hard in the carton and when I take them out of the carton I take the cellophane wrapper off each box and I open the lid and take that one little silver paper out, because I know I'll have to do that eventually, so to save time I do all ten at once, throw them down the toilet and put the cigarettes in the drawer, so when I go to get a pack of cigarettes, I don't have that to do any more. Sometimes, I smoke just to make space in my cigarette container. Anyway, I'm always photographing whatever I put in the toilet and then I photographed when I peed. To give it a good effect, I like to wipe myself and then throw the cigarette I was smoking between my legs – I burned myself once that way. And I throw the cigarettes into the toilet because I'm always trying to stop smoking.

'And I throw out the covers of *Oui* so the hotel manager won't know it's a dirty magazine. I throw out things I don't want people to see.'

'Can you hold on,' I interrupted, rather politely I thought. I could have just put the receiver down quietly and snook away. 'I have to go pee.'

'I can't, A.'

'Okay, hold on.'

I ran to the bathroom – and ran back. 'Okay,' I said.

'I'll tell you another thing,' B said. 'I don't like to go to the john any place but here. I'd rather come all the way home to go and then go back. But at some point I really have to.'

'That's just like me,' I said, wondering if way-back-when picked up this idea from B or she picked it up from me.

'Anyway, last night I walked across the street to the deli and bought a sandwich, a beer, a cake, frozen cake, orange, Sara Lee, some ice cream. Came home, ate the sandwich with my coat still on because I wanted to throw away the paper it came in and drank the beer, too, so I could throw away the bottle. Then I thought I couldn't wait for the cake to defrost. I really didn't want butter pecan ice cream, I wanted Haägen-Dazs new honey ice cream but they didn't have it. Of course I couldn't wait for the ice cream to pour or the cake to thaw so I chewed them both. I'm so edgy that just waiting for the elevator drives me crazy. I still have a quarter of the orange cake left and all I want to do is throw out the plate, so maybe I can become undepressed right now if I flush the cake down the toilet and don't eat, to throw out the plate. I can prove right now that cleaning is more important than eating to me. I flush the cake down the toilet and put the tin box in the waste basket. Now I have to get dressed to take the basket out because it has something in it. The silver tin won't flush. It just floats on top. A number of times I've gotten really nervous because I've had a flood. What I was flushing down was "pokers", because I got very nervous and thought, "Today they're going to get me." I got nervous and flushed. Well, the plastic poker flushed but the sewing equipment stayed at the bottom right near the hole. They didn't flush. You can throw all your needlepoint needles down the toilet and they don't go down, they just sit there at the bottom. Well, I had to fish them out. So I had to put on the yellow lined gloves again and it was very hard with rubber gloves to pick up the needles. So I put — first, I put more Comet in to make the toilet clean and some Sani-Flush and I flushed again, I knew the needle wasn't going to go down, so I had to pick it up and put it in a Marlboro box, and I knew that the Marlboro box always goes down, so I put the needle in and out like I was sewing it. In the cardboard. And wrapped it up and it went down and my worries were gone. Then all of a sudden the toilet started to bubble. And when I flushed it again it went up to the rim. It didn't really go over the rim; it just stayed there. I could have dived in. You know? I said, "Oh, I don't have a plunger and I'm broke." I called the engineer. I said, "John, I can't understand it, my toilet's overflowing." He came up here and he said, "Was it anything?" And I knew it was not like what any other girl would probably worry over, like a Tampax. I was just scared about the Marlboro box, because I knew that if it came back up it would be all soggy and there would be the sewing equipment visible right there. Then nothing seemed to come up and he asked me what I'd put in there and I said, "Nothing, maybe a lot of toilet paper and a bar of soap, I think." Because I always put the soap in when the Yardley's gets down to very small. I don't dig small cakes of soap. Anyway, he's plunging and I'm thinking of all the things that are going to come up. Well, I'm asking him questions about where does it all go, because all of the stuff that I've flushed for the last ten years was probably going to back up in my toilet just then. I wonder where it really does go. I flushed as a child too. I flushed everything I didn't want my mother to see. Flushing doesn't take as long as burning. Now, you can burn a letter with dirty words up in an ashtray. But God it takes so many matches just to do that little thing when you can just flush it. Anyway, after I clean my room I still have to clean my body. I don't really have any set routine of getting up and taking a bath in the morning or taking a bath at night because I can get up any time, clean any time, vacuum, flush – I just do it when I'm in the mood. My bath can be at night, in the afternoon, or in the morning. But before I take it, I have to know that I'm well stocked. With everything I'm going to need. I used to really love creams. I used to go to drugstores and spend a hundred dollars on all these different eye moisturizers and under-eye creams and all that total junk, and I realized that when I put it under my eyes when I went to sleep, I'd wake up and my lashes would be stuck together with crust on them and everything, and I kind of just began to get simpler, to eliminate some products, and yet I still just have to buy every new thing I see. I use this stuff called Time Spa, which comes in a big jar and it's a dollar ninety-five. And yet I also go and buy the essence of the same stuff which is much more expensive and comes in little packets. First I put that in the tub. I use half the jar, it's like a quart jar. I run lukewarm water in the bathtub. And I get in when the water is a quarter filled. Because when I get in, you see, it goes up pretty high. So I don't want to waste the stuff, you know? So I get in and lie flat down in the tub with my legs sort of up because I really can't fit in the tub that well. I'd sent away for this pillow on a box of Q-tips – "Send-Away-Pillow-for-the-Bathtub." And

I thought I'd get a yellow one. So I blew it up and I suction-cupped it to the back of my tub so I can lay flat in the tub and rub hot water on me. The first thing I start to wash is my shoulders. I haven't gotten my hair wet yet, and I'm still lying down, and I've put an old ratty scarf around my head. Just so I can relax and get my neck clean. Because I'm going to take a shower after this anyway, to rinse this bath off. So I just start with my left arm, that's the first thing I scrub with my terry mitt that I put my whole hand in, then I scrub my chest, then I scrub my left leg and my left foot. I hate this foot business, because it means reaching down or lifting up, it means bringing the foot up to my mouth or sitting up in the tub like I'm at the typewriter and bending down to wash my feet. First I do it with the mitt. Then I use a vegetable brush. And I scrub like hell the soles of my feet. Then I use pumice stones called Weiss. I used to use Dr Scholl's pumice stones but they had sulphur and the smell was so disgusting I'd have to let the tub out again just after doing my feet because there'd be all these little flakes of black stuff from the sulphur. So I found this thing called Weiss. It's German and you let if float in the water for a second, let it get soft. First I pumice-stone my heels, and up the sides of my feet, and then my toes. Then after I've done that to both feet, I'm all totally out of breath and I have to lie back again. I *still* have to go through the thing of reaching again and going up and down because the razor is at the end of the tub near where the faucet is. And every time I take a bath I take the razor, and I put a little soap under my arms and I shave down under both arms. Then I squat down further in the tub so my leg is sort of touching the pole in the shower and I start to shave my legs. I kind of rub them with soap, a little loose soap and water, and then I shave the hair on my legs, and then I shave the hair on both big toes. And then I open up the razor and run lukewarm water over it, because I once found a razor where the hair was stuck to the blade and it made me sick. I don't ever touch my face in the bathtub. Then I wash my cunt. I kind of lie there. I do that with my mitt too. And if I have a Tampax in I have to stand up again, in the tub, and pull it out. Because even if I have my period I want to pull the Tampax out and still do a good scrubbing. I mean, I don't scrub up inside or anything like that, but I do scrub on the outside. I scrub my fanny, but I don't get anal. I don't go in there for a separate operation. I know it's getting clean just sitting in the water. Then I always put the soap right back. I hate soap when you get it out of the soap dish and it has gotten all soft and slimy. That makes me throw up. Then I just lie there for another ten seconds and I let the water out of the tub. Then I decide, well, since I've gotten the end of my hair a little wet, I may as well wash it. I move the yellow bathroom rug that's hanging over the top of the shower because I don't want it to get dirty because then I'd have to take it to the laundry. I get under the shower and with lukewarm water I just wet my hair and then I wring it a little bit and then I decide which shampoo I'm going to use. I get a nice lather up and I massage my head with my fingers really great. Near my temples. And then up at the top of my head. Then I rinse with lukewarm water which I let get colder and colder and colder. So then my hair is rinsed and I just take like a big blob of water in my hand, like a cup, and I splash that on my cunt and make sure all the soap is off. Then I turn the water off and I take the green – because my bathroom's yellow and green – I take the green sponge and wring it out. I always have to sponge down the ConTact paper on the wall because it begins to peel off, so I sponge from the ceiling all the way down, then I sponge the chrome bar, and then I look at that and get really depressed because there's some rust on it, and then I do the walls just to get them dry. Then I bend down outside the shower because now there's a big puddle where the water's gone and I sop that up and then I squeeze the sponge back in the tub. Then I put a white mat on the floor, put a towel around my head, tie it in a knot, and then I sort of shake myself a little bit – I like to do a kind of bird motion with my arms. And then I put on my yellow soft terry-cloth bathrobe. I learned that from the French husband of a friend. And then I use a whole brand new towel, I just stick it between my legs. You know? Then I get the hairdryer out and turn the air conditioner off. So I don't blow a fuse. Then

I plug the hairdryer in and I stand in the bathroom with my legs apart, and I hold the dryer and I dry my pubic hairs. But I'm more interested really in drying the insides of my thighs. Because if they're at all wet and I put my underpants on and walk around with wet between my thighs, I can't stand it. It really hurts. When it's completely dry I just take a little bit of baby powder and with my hands softly put a little on. And then I have a comb that's like a comb for the purse. And I just sort of fluff up the pubic hairs a little. But then I never finish, because I always think, "My God, why am I bothering to fluff them up so they come as far out as my stomach?" And every two months or so when I feel they're getting a little long I take regular art shears and clip maybe an eighth of an inch off so it's always neat. I did it once too much and it itched terribly. I walked down the street and it was just insane. A, are you there? Are you bored?'

'No.'

'No, I know, because this is important. Cleanliness counts, it interests you, you believe in it, I know. So – then I look at all my hairs and start to wish they would *all* go gray in a year. I think how beautiful it would be to be Prematurely Gray. But then I remember, "You think you're going to be prematurely gray but you're mature already."'

B was so involved in our conversation I figured I could make a quick dash to the kitchen to switch from apple butter to orange marmalade.

'. . . on a Sunday and the stores aren't open. And Brentano's in the Village isn't open yet and I don't feel like goofing next door in Azuma's with the wicker laundry baskets until Brentano's opens. And I know that the man I don't like is on duty at Bigelow's Pharmacy on Sixth Avenue. So what I do is I put the immersion coil in my cup and plug it in, and then I take a spiced teabag and I put it in the cup, and when it cools off I wash my face with the tea. That makes my skin very firm and takes away the wrinkles. Then after I take the tea off I decide to give myself a masque, and there's a coffee masque – this is the newest one that Revlon's make – a coffee-musk masque. It's really strange to feel a masque drying hard on my face. I put the egg-timer on so I know when to take the masque off because I like to hear the little bell. I either use the coffee-musk masque or the egg masque or the medicated masque, or the old-fashioned masque. The first masque I ever used had a very famous name I can't remember, well anyway, it was a mud-pack. And I used to do that in the country, but I got to thinking that it couldn't be good for your skin, sticking all that damn mud on it. And I thought, "I'm certainly not going to henna myself. That's all I need with the size of my body – henna hair." Then, oh, then, sometimes I plug my vibrator in. This is after I've set my hair and everything and I'm still working on a few things while I'm nude. Since I can only see down to my breastbone in both of my mirrors I feel like I need a massage on my shoulders. So I take the vibrator out. And I put on the legitimate attachment, you know, not the little tiny suction-cup attachment that, you know . . .'

I tip-toed back to the phone and picked up the receiver very carefully. B usually hears me doing this but today was special, she was talking about the subject she's most involved in, keeping clean.

'. . . and then I rub a little bit of turtle oil into my shoulders. Okay, sometimes I actually use Ben-Gay. Or else, hold on, I'll tell you what it's called . . .'

I couldn't believe it, B was running off and leaving me with nothing to listen to. That's the problem, she gets so involved in whatever she's talking about she sometimes forgets that it takes two to . . .

'. . . Here it is, it's called Exercaine External Analgesic and Anesthetic Spray and I just love it. I spray that on my shoulders, I really massage it in. And then I have to clean the vibrator and everything because I don't want the smell of Exercaine in the bag I keep the vibrator in. The only cream I keep in the vibrator bag is old-fashioned Elizabeth Arden cleansing cream. Funnily enough, that's the best. Now, if I've set my hair and it's all sprayed crisp, it's already beginning to droop and fall apart at the center. So then I have to run around the top of my bureau drawer and put it up in what I call my "Debbie". And my "Debbie" is just like a Yorkshire terrier tuft on top. I used to use rubber bands just so my hair wouldn't fall in my eyes. And I'm all neat and my blush-on is on and everything and I've massaged my shoulders with the vibrator and put the vibrator back into its bag. It's a little European makeup bag. Striped. Green and pink stripes. So the vibrator is back in the bag. But the sight of that bag. I keep looking at that bag. I think to myself, "Oh, well, why not?" So I pull the blinds down. If I don't have two C-batteries alkaline on hand, I call the bellman and I say, "Will you please go across the street to the camera store and bring me up two C-batteries alkaline." Then while he's waiting for me to pay him I test them with my little professional battery tester. Then I pay him, tip him, he leaves, and I'm all set . . .'

I was beginning to doze off. B was talking about how since 1968 every time she had sex with someone she taped it and now she uses those tapes for atmosphere when she needs it. She went on and on describing the way she caters to her more personal needs but I only heard phrases between snoozes.

'. . . long or short session . . . afternoon quickie? . . . Arden cream . . . four pieces of Kleenex . . . come simultaneously with the tape . . . remote-control button . . . try to be quiet . . . decided there's nowhere to go . . . just take another bath afterwards . . . *machine du massage* in Paris . . . had the current changed from two-twenty to one-twenty . . . reading the stories with my left hand . . . forgot the "Don't Disturb" sign . . . strung it through a wire coat-hanger . . . in one of the loops of the radiator . . . waiting to be electrocuted . . . what if my mother found me like that . . . rest of her life would be a trauma . . . Tiffany blue . . . too prudish to buy the really big size, now I'm sorry . . .'

The doorbell rang and I snapped up and ran off to answer it. When I returned to the phone B was in a state of panic.

'A? . . . A? . . . A! You really freak me out when you leave me! A? A? A?'

'Hello? I had to answer the door.'

'How could you? A, you know how much our phone calls mean to me. Eye contact is the worst contact to have with somebody – I don't care about *that*. Ear contact is so much better. This morning talking to you about all these things is just like the old days. I don't see anything in people really. I just hear things in them. But when you walk away from the phone it freaks me out. When you go off to another part of the house with the delivery boy or the plumber, I get really upset.'

B paused. I guess she was upset because it was her first pause in an hour.

'I wonder if the pigeon on my windowsill knows what I'm doing,' she said, when she caught her breath.

'Probably.'

'I'm out of cream.'

'That's okay, B. I have to go.'

15 **Underwear Power**

Buying is much more American than thinking and I'm as American as they come. In Europe and the Orient people like to trade – buy and sell, sell and buy – they're basically merchants. Americans are not so interested in selling – in fact, they'd rather throw out than sell. What they really like to do is buy – people, money, countries.

Saturday is the big buying – or 'shopping' – day in America and I look forward to it as much as the next guy.

My favorite thing to buy is underwear. I think buying underwear is the most personal thing you can do, and if you could watch a person buying underwear you would really get to know them. I mean, I would rather watch somebody buy their underwear than read a book they wrote. I think the strangest people are the ones who send someone else to buy their underwear for them. I also wonder about people who *don't* buy underwear. I can understand not wearing it, but not buying it?

Anyway, one Saturday morning I called a B who knows me pretty well and asked him if he would like to go underwear-shopping with me at Macy's.

'Macy's?' he grumbled. I guess I woke him up but think of all the buying time he was losing. 'Why Macy's?'

'Because that's where I get my underwear,' I told him. I used to go to Woolworth's but now I can afford Macy's. Periodically I stop in at Brooks Brothers to look at their fancy old-fashioned boxer shorts but I just can't bring myself to give up Jockeys.

'I wouldn't mind buying some underwear,' B said, 'but I buy mine at Bloomingdale's. They have pure cotton. Pima cotton.' This B is like that. He finds something he likes, Pima cotton for example, and he acts like he discovered it. He gets completely attached to it. He won't buy anything else. He has extremely definite taste. Which I think is bad because it limits his buying power.

'No, let's go to Macy's.'

'Saks is nice,' he whimpered.

'Macy's,' I insisted. 'I'll pick you up in an hour.'

I need about an hour to glue myself together, but when I make an appointment I always forget about the phone call interruptions so I always show up a little late, and a little unglued. B was waiting for me on his corner.

'You're fifteen minutes late,' he said, climbing into the taxi.

'Herald Square,' I said to the driver.

'It's going to be hell on Saturday,' said B.

'I was on the phone,' I said. 'Paul Morrissey called. Ingrid Superstar called. Jackie Curtis called. Franco Rossellini called. Oh look, who's that? Is that someone we know?' A four-foot-two old lady was crossing Park Avenue at 65th Street. She had frizzy red hair and was wearing black gloves, a pink sweater, a black dress, red shoes, and she was carrying a red bag. She was hunchbacked. I don't know why, but she seemed like someone we would know. But B didn't recognize her so I didn't bother to roll down the window and wave.

I asked B once and for all if he was going to buy any underwear and he said no, not at Macy's because he only liked Bloomingdale's Pima cotton or Saks Fifth Avenue's own brand. This B is really stubborn.

'Do you think Howard Hughes wears underwear?' I asked B. 'Do you think he washes it or throws it away after he wears it once?' He probably throws new suits away. What I've always really wished I'd invented was paper underwear, even knowing that the idea never took off when they did come out with it. I still think it's a good idea, and I don't know why people resist it when they've accepted paper napkins and paper plates and paper curtains and paper towels – it would make more sense not to have to wash out underwear than not to have to wash out towels.

B said he might consider buying a couple of pairs of socks, because 'socks just disappear'. He doesn't wash his own, of course, he sends them to a very fancy East Side French dry cleaner's and

212

they still come back with one missing. It really is a law – the diminishing return of socks.

The reason I hate regular underwear – and socks, too – is that if you send twenty pairs of shorts and twenty pairs of socks to the laundromat, you always only get nineteen back. Even when I wash them myself, I get nineteen back. The more I think about it, the more I can't believe the diminishing returns on underwear. It's unbelievable. I WASH MY OWN AND I STILL GET NINETEEN BACK!

I wash my own, and I put them in myself, and I take them out myself, and I put them in the dryer myself, and then I go through the dryer feeling around all the holes and ridges looking for the missing sock, and I never find it! I go up and down the stairs looking for it, thinking it fell, but I never find it! It's like a law of physics . . .

I told B I needed some socks too and at least thirty pairs of Jockey shorts. He suggested I switch to Italian-style briefs, the ones with the t-shaped crotch that tends to build you up. I told him I'd tried them once, in Rome, the day I was walking through a Liz Taylor movie – and I didn't like them because they made me too self-aware. It gave me the feeling girls must have when they wear uplift bras.

Suddenly B said, 'There's your first Superstar.'

'Who? Ingrid?'

'The Empire State Building.' We had just turned into 34th Street. He laughed at his own joke while I fished around my boot for a couple of singles to pay the taxi.

At Herald Square people were pouring into Macy's from all over the world. At least they looked like they came from all over the world. But they were all Americans and though they had lots of different color skins they all had buying in their blood and minds and eyes. People look so determined entering a department store. B, naturally, turned his upturned nose up and began to go straight to the men's department.

I was getting annoyed. I don't come to Macy's that often and I wanted to take my time shopping through it. 'Don't rush me, B.'

I wanted to check out the price tags on the plastic bags and see if they had gone up much since last time. I hear all this talk about 'inflation' and I wanted to see for myself if it was true.

'It's so mobbed,' B whined.

It *was* crowded, especially for a Saturday in summer. 'Shouldn't all these people be away?' I asked.

'These kind of people don't go away,' B said, very snottily I thought

I stopped and watched a Japanese lady in a kimono make up an American lady in a jumpsuit. They were starring in 'Shiseido Presents Exotic Makeup Artist for Free'. Then we walked past the big Charlie promotion, past the Famous Maker Ties, past the candy department – which took a lot of willpower on my part. I walked past the Raspberry-Cherry Mix-Max, the Licorice All-Kinds, the Jelly Beans, the Rock Candy, the Chocolate Pretzels, the TV Munch, the Petit Fours, the Mon Cherry, the Lollipops, the Nonpareils, I even walked past the Whitman Samplers. The smell of chocolate was driving me nuts but I didn't say a word. I didn't even sigh or moan. I just thought of my pimples and gall bladder and kept on walking.

'Where *is* the men's department, B?' I finally asked. We were entering Cigars.

'This is the World's Largest Store,' B said, as if I didn't know. 'We have to walk all the way from Sixth Avenue to Seventh Avenue. But we're getting closer – here's Men's Sunglasses.'

Men's Sunglasses led to Men's Scarves which led to Men's Pajamas and then – then! – Men's Underwear, I quickly found the brand I usually use, Jockey Classic Briefs. They were three for five dollars which didn't seem too inflationary. I read the label on the plastic bag they came in, just to make sure they hadn't changed any of their famous 'Comfort Features' – 'Exclusive Tailoring for Proper Fit to Support a Man's Needs; Contoured Designed Arch Gives Added Comfort No Gaps; Support Waistband is Smoother Fitted Heat Resistant; Stronger Longer Lasting "V" No Chafe Leg Openings; Soft Rubber at Either Thigh Only; Highly Absorbent 100 Per Cent Highly Combed Cotton.'

So far so good, I thought. I checked the 'Washing Instructions' –
'Machine Wash Tumble Dry.' Everything was fine, the same as
always. I hate it when you find a product you like that fits a
particular need of yours, and then they change it. 'Improve' it. I
hate 'new, improved' anything. I think they should just make a
completely new product instead and leave the old one alone. That
way there would be two products to choose from, instead of half
an old one. At least the Jockey Classic Briefs were still Classic,
but before I committed myself to buying them I decided to ask
the saleslady to show me what else was available on the underwear
market. This saleslady was pleasantly plump in her neat navy-blue
shirtwaist dress with a red-and-white scarf tied around her
double chin. She had a nice smile and eyeglasses with rhinestones
sprayed around the frames. She looked like the type you could
feel comfortable talking about underwear with.

'Do you have BVDs?' I asked.

She pushed her eyeglasses further up her nose, right up to the
ridge, and she said, 'No, we don't carry BVDs.'

'Does Macy's make its own brand, like Saks?' B piped up. Who
was he trying to impress? The saleslady?

'Certainly. We have Macy's Supremacy right here.' She lifted
a package to show me. 'They're two for five dollars.'

'Two for five dollars! These are *three* for five dollars,' I
exclaimed. I had some Jockeys in my hand.

'Well, Supremacy is the better line. They fit better. We also
have Macy's Kenton. They're three for four-fifty.'

She handed me a package of Kentons. 'This is all cotton too,' I
said.

'There are different *grades* of cotton, you know,' she said.

I was confused. I looked at the Supremacy package more closely.
'What's this? "Swiss Rib Side Panels?" Does that make it better?'

'That,' said the saleslady, 'and the quality of the cotton.'

'But what *are* "Swiss Rib Side Panels"?'

'How do I know? It makes them fit better,' she said grimly.
'What brand do you generally use? BVD?'

'Jockey.'

'Jockey!' There was a note of triumph in her voice now. 'Supremacy is cut longer than Jockey. It's a longer brief. But if you like the Jockey cut I would suggest you stick to it.'

'How many pairs should I get?' I mumbled to B. There was no point asking the saleslady to show me anything else. She had made up my mind when she made up hers. 'I need about twenty-eight.'

'You can't get twenty-eight if there are three in a package,' B explained. 'You can get twenty-seven or thirty but not twenty-eight.'

'Okay then, I'll take fifteen.'

'Cash or charge,' said the saleslady.

'Cash,' I said. I don't like charging. It feels more like buying if you pay with money. The saleslady went off to ring the sale up. Another saleslady, who looked a lot like her, came up to us and asked, 'Are you together?'

'Are we together?' I asked B.

'Yes,' B said, a bit annoyed. The second saleslady walked away. 'Look at these Jockey Thoroughbred Nylon Briefs.' B pointed to an adjacent rack.

'Are they better?'

'You can use them as a bathing suit,' B said. The saleslady returned with my change. 'We have one over here,' she said, 'that's supposed to be used as a bathing suit. Let me show it to you.'

We followed her down a narrow aisle lined with more kinds of underwear than I knew existed.

'Here,' she said, handing B a package of Pucci-looking bikini underwear.

'Are they Jockey?' I asked.

'JockeyLife.'

'Do they come in any other colors?'

'They come in a print called Balloons,' she said, handing me a package of blue-and-green JockeyLife bikinis.

'Don't they come in white?'

'No they don't but we have these others over here by Jockey –

216

Jockey Skins. Now *they* come in white, but they are not as brief.'

I examined the package, trying to imagine myself in Jockey Skins instead of Jockey Classic Briefs. But I just couldn't, so I handed the package back to her and thanked her for her help.

As we walked through the further reaches of the Men's Underwear department, it hit me that B and I were the only men in the whole department. And it wasn't empty. There were women everywhere. At first I wondered if women now were buying men's underwear just like they buy men's jeans and men's sweaters but then I saw that these were all middle-aged married-looking women shopping for their husbands. I guess that's what marriage boils down to – your wife buys your underwear for you.

B had detoured into the exotic underwear aisle – the mesh g-string aisle – and was having a good time reading the labels. 'Look at this one,' he said. 'It says "Horizontal fly for easy access." '

'Strange,' I said. 'Why do they have a pocket in the pouch?'

'That's the horizontal fly for easy access.' B chuckled. 'Here's one that says "Exclusive for easy convenience." '

'Come on, let's go, I have to buy some socks,' I said.

The Men's Socks department was bustling with women too. Maybe that's what's wrong with America. The men don't buy.

'Where are the SuppHose?' I asked B.

'You wear SuppHose?' B said. 'Do you have arthritis?' I don't have arthritis but I want to be ready for it when it comes. I also like SuppHose because they are very tight and that leaves more space between my leg and my boot for money. I found the SuppHose rack and read the label on one of the boxes – 'New No-Static Anti-Static All-Nylon'. I was a little disturbed by the 'New'. I asked B to call for a salesman. He found one around the corner, straightening out the Camp socks rack, and brought him over to me. The salesman was very tall, his hair was very short, and he was wearing a three-piece dacron-polyester olive-green twill suit, a bright-green Rooster tie, a yellow wash-and-wear shirt – more worn than washed – and Hush Puppies. His cologne smelled like Hai Karate but it could have been Jade East. He smiled tentatively.

'Why does it say "New" on this package?' I asked him.

'Those are two-tone, sir, something new SuppHose has come out with.' His smile was still pretty tentative.

'No,' I declared, 'I want solids.'

'All right, sir. In solids we have a choice of four colors – black, brown, navy blue, and medium gray.'

'May I see the navy blue, please?'

'Here's navy blue. It looks dark but the light is different here than outside.'

'Maybe I should stick with black. How many pairs do you have here?' I poked around the rack looking for stray pairs of black, size small.

'Sir, we have eight here, but I can get you as many as you'd like.'

'Eight's enough.' I didn't want him taking a cigarette break in the stockroom on my time. 'And, please take them out of the boxes. They're hard to carry.'

His tentative smile faded. 'Sir, they're on cardboards.'

'That's okay. Just take them out of the boxes. You don't have to take the cardboards out.'

'The only thing I would say, sir, is if for any reason you want to return them you can't if they're not in their boxes.'

'No, I won't return them.' I never return anything. That's worse than not buying.

The salesman began to take them out of their boxes. When he was on number seven, I asked, 'Is there any other brand?'

'There's one other brand we carry, sir – Mandate. It's not as effective. But it *is* less expensive.'

'No,' I said.

Just then B came back from buying a bunch of socks for himself in various dark, respectable colors – navy, brown, forest green, charcoal, black.

'Why do you buy different color socks, B?'

218

'So they're easy to separate when they're washed.'

'But if you get all the same color you can put any one with any other one.'

We paid for our socks and walked on through Macy's. It really was crowded and noisy and much less like a museum than Bloomingdale's. I suggested a little lunch somewhere in the store.

'Lunch in a department store?' B was absolutely horrified, as if I had suggested sending out to a sewer or something. He really is a spoiled brat, a product of postwar affluence.

'Okay B, we'll have lunch in a hotel uptown.' B smiled; he was as pleased as he could ever be pleased. 'But first let's go to Gimbel's. They might have some old jewelry. They buy estates.'

Outside it really hit me that New York isn't Paris. Thirty-fourth Street was crawling with potential muggers, potential rapists, potential degenerates, potential murderers. There were very few potential victims in sight.

'Let's cut through Woolworth's to 33rd Street and Gimbel's,' I said. I used to buy my underwear at Woolworth's so I have a sentimental attachment to it. The first thing you notice when you enter Woolworth's is the smell of fried chicken frying. It smelled so good I almost bought some even though I don't like fried chicken. In high-class stores they sell through 'display', in low-class ones they sell through 'smell'. B of course had his nose wrinkled up and was rushing right through.

'Why are you rushing, B?'

'That buzz is driving me crazy.'

'What buzz?' I listened and there was a buzz, probably a faulty air-conditioning system, but for me it was completely drowned out by the smell of roasted peanuts. 'Aren't you glad you were born rich, B?' B is just not the five-and-dime type, so he's lucky he wasn't born into a five-and-dime family.

We were almost at the 33rd Street side of Woolworth's, where they have those 3-D postcards of the World Trade Center and the Spanish-speaking greeting cards. We exited and crossed the street and entered Gimbel's. It was as crowded and noisy as Macy's. B groaned. 'Can't we look for old jewelry at Cartier's?'

'Cartier's!' I was really getting angry with B. 'Listen, B, I think
we should do this every day, it would do you a lot of good,
coming out into the world and seeing what life is all about. It
doesn't start at Saks and end at Bloomingdale's. It's not a YSL
boutique. Maybe you should spend more time getting underwear
and socks and going to the dime store.' B grimaced. 'This is what
real life is, B!' I turned away from B in disgust and noticed two
little girls, about ten and twelve, rustling through a drawer of
tee-shirts. 'Those little kids are shoplifting!' I shouted.

'That's how much you know about the real world,' said B.
'Didn't you ever just open drawers when you were a kid to see if
they had different things from on top of the counters?'

'No.'

'I used to open drawers and find different colors and sizes and
styles. Anyway, what's wrong with shoplifting? Didn't you ever
shoplift?'

'No.' I couldn't be bothered with B. I had just discovered the
In and Out Shop – Gimbel's version of a 'head' shop. I was
contemplating buying it out – every last piece of fake stained
glass, every Mexican silver bracelet, every Kama Sutra poster,
every daisy-decal mirror, every peacock feather. This is what
people will probably be collecting in the 80s. Art-à-Go-Go. The
60s Plastic-Psychedelic look. There won't be any 20s, 30s, 40s, or
50s stuff left.

B was rushing off to the school-supplies department. 'Did you
used to get a new lunchbox and briefcase and looseleaf and pencils
every September? That was my favorite time of year. It was really
exciting dividing the looseleaf into different sections with a
different color for each subject. I could never decide which
bookcover look I liked better, the shiny Ivy League covers from
the drugstore or the plain brown papersack- covers you made
yourself. Did you have book covers, A?'

'For what?'

'For school.'

'No.'

I asked a passing salesgirl for directions to Used Jewelry and she told me it was right past Cosmetics. We walked on. 'Shiseido Presents Exotic Makeup Artist for Free' was also playing at Gimbel's.

At the first-floor jewelry department, a sign said, 'End of the Season Gold Clearance – 20 to 50% off.' I wondered which season was the Gold season. The single salesman there was helping a customer try on a ring. 'How does that one feel?' he asked.

'Tight,' said the customer.

As much as I hate to cut in on a purchase, I did. 'Where's your used jewelry?'

'The used jewelry would be on the fifth floor.'

B and I headed for the escalator. On the way up I noticed Robert Redford on the way down. 'Look, B, there's Robert Redford.' Maybe it wasn't Robert Redford. But he was wearing a white suit and had sandy blond hair and a big smile.

'My sister saw Robert Redford on Madison Avenue the other day,' B said.

'I saw him the other day too. He must be in town.'

'My sister followed him up Madison.'

'I followed him in a cab.'

'He lives on Fifth Avenue.'

'I followed him on Park Avenue, from 64th Street to 65th Street. He was walking too slow for my cab to keep up with him, so I lost him.'

'My sister said nobody recognized him.'

'I know, I was the only one following him on Park Avenue . . .' We were just arriving at the third floor and there was a seersucker suit on a mannequin that looked like Robert Redford.

'I come out of a department store,' B was saying as we headed up to four, 'feeling like I've been hit over the head. I only like small shops. Big stores take too much out of you.'

'But you can get bargains in big stores.'

'If you have the patience to look. But just think of the time it's costing you.'

At the fifth floor the used jewelry department was right near the escalator. There were two counters, sparkling with diamonds, rubies, emeralds, gold, silver. On the first counter everything looked new. I asked the salesman if he had any jewelry from the 40s. He said no. 'Do you have an old counter?' I persisted.

'We have nothing there, either,' he said.

I approached the salesman behind the second counter. He saw me coming and looked down and pretended to be writing in his order book.

'Excuse me.' He didn't look up. 'I'm looking for used jewelry. Do you have any?' He still didn't look up. 'I read your ad.' He finally looked up and said, 'No.'

'Well, you have an Estate Sale, according to the ad.' I never had to work so hard to buy in my life.

'What we have is all mixed up,' he said. 'We don't keep everything in one case.' He waved his arm across the counter. I looked down through the glass. A very simple three-color gold cigarette case caught my eye.

'How much is that?' I asked. 'Is it on sale?'

'No.'

'Why not?'

'It wasn't advertised.'

'Well, what else is there? I'm looking for something with a big stone. A big, big stone.'

'There are some rings over there. You might see something you like.'

I looked.

'Remember,' B said, 'how big that amethyst we saw in Paris was. How purple. It was Siberian, not South American. It belonged to the Imperial Family.' As B talked the Gimbel's jewels looked smaller and smaller.

There was one gold-and-diamond brooch in the 40s style I liked because it reminded me of the good old days.

'May I see this one?'

'This one?' said the salesman, picking it up as if it were a black widow spider.

'Is it signed by any name?'

'No.'

222

'Is this a good diamond?'

'Is it a good diamond?' Suddenly the black widow was a butterfly. 'Yes, sir. This is a very good buy. This is an Estate Piece. There are two carats of diamonds in here.'

'Let's go, B,' I whispered. 'This guy is awful.' As we headed toward the escalator I overheard a customer ask the salesman at the other counter, 'You mean you might not have another one for three years?'

'That's right. Come back in three years.'

'But will the price be the same?'

'I don't know if the price'll be the same *tomorrow*.'

I stepped on the escalator, frustrated that a salesman had kept me from buying.

'How come you like jewelry so much, A?' B asked.

'I don't like jewelry that much. Let's go buy some Dr Scholl's Footsavers. Jewelry will never replace Dr Scholl's.'

'I'd rather have jewelry,' B said.

'Why?'

'Because a diamond is forever,' B said.

'Forever what?'

Ladies and Gentlemen — Lenny Bruce!! £1.50

Albert Goldman from the journalism of Lawrence Schiller

'Every once in a while a *real* book comes along; one that in style, comprehensiveness, frankness, responsibility of research, emotional and intellectual sting rises far above the genre. *Ladies and Gentlemen — Lenny Bruce!!* is exhaustive — affairs, patter, technique, habits, neuroses, finances, drug addiction and court battles of the late great standup comic. It's the compleat Lenny... a haunting book with countless vivid scenes, mostly nightmarish, that threaten to distort the mind in some scary, permanent way'
NEW YORK MAGAZINE

'Short of the living Bruce himself, this book is the next best thing'
NEW YORK TIMES

'An extraordinary book' SUNDAY TIMES

Tom Wolfe
The New Journalism £1.50

'A galaxy of world wide journalistic talent... Truman Capote inside the mind of a psychotic killer; Terry Southern exploring the strange rituals of the baton-twirlers; Rex Reed giving the star treatment to the ageing Ava Gardner... Hunter S. Thompson, Norman Mailer, Nicholas Tomalin and many other wizards of tape and typewriter — telling it like it is from the Vietnam backwoods to the White House Lawn.

You can buy these and other Picador Books from booksellers and newsagents; or direct from the following address:
Pan Books, Sales Office, Cavaye Place, London SW10 9PG
Send purchase price plus 20p for the first book and 10p for each additional book, to allow for postage and packing
Prices quoted are applicable in the UK

While every effort is made to keep prices low, it is sometimes necessary to increase prices at short notice. Pan Books reserve the right to show on covers and charge new retail prices which may differ from those advertised in the text or elsewhere